STRETCHING
BEYOND
THE TEXTBOOK

READING AND SUCCEEDING WITH COMPLEX TEXTS IN THE CONTENT AREAS

LAUREN K. FRANCESE & REBECCA H. MARSICK

SCHOLASTIC

New York • Toronto • London • Auckland • Sydney
Mexico City • New Delhi • Hong Kong • Buenos Aires

DEDICATION

For our families

ACKNOWLEDGMENTS

The ideas presented in this book would have never left our classrooms were it not for the support of a number of distinguished professionals.

First and foremost, there are a few people who recognized the potential of our ideas in their infancy. We owe a debt of gratitude to Joanna Davis-Swing, our enthusiastic and supportive development editor, who saw MINDful reading presented in front of an audience of no more than a dozen people and wanted to make it a book. Sacred Heart University professor Richard Carmelich was the guiding force behind a data-driven investigation that showed how truly effective this strategy could be. Without his endless edits and commitment to action research, the potential of this work might have gone unnoticed. Our editor, Sarah Glasscock, is also a deeply appreciated critical friend who worked with us to make sure our ideas were articulated for our readers.

Second, we have several colleagues to thank for their inspiration, motivation, and support. Courtney Ruggiero was willing to implement social studies MIND units and give feedback from the moment she walked into Bedford Middle School; her commitment to thoughtful instruction is unmatched. Dan Cortright embraced cross-disciplinary work and inspired the science connections throughout this book; he is the most enthusiastic collaborator on the planet. Lynn Fay was a mentor and supporter throughout this process. April Harvey and Jane Silvestro have been invaluable resources for brainstorming nonfiction strategies, especially for students with special needs. Alison Laturnau and Kerry-Jean Douglas gladly joined us for collaborative planning throughout the years, and their honest and humorous feedback always kept us motivated. James D'Amico, Megan Tiley, and Anthony Formato were our fearless leaders throughout this entire process. We thank them for finding a way to make resources available and placing the highest priority on best practices in our classrooms. And thank you to all of our Westport colleagues for a deep commitment to excellence.

Finally, many thanks belong to the Westport Public Schools, especially Elliott Landon and Lis Comm, for their efforts to develop a rich and dynamic curriculum.

● ● ● ● ●

Cover design: Jorge J. Namerow
Interior design: Sarah Morrow
Development Editor: Joanna Davis-Swing
Editor: Sarah Glasscock
Copyeditor: David Klein

ISBN: 978-0-545-55490-9

Contents

Introduction

With the advent of the Common Core State Standards (CCSS), it is time for educators to stretch beyond the textbook. Rich and dynamic reading materials are the key to engaging students in the deep reading and thinking that these new standards require. We have developed the MIND methods and strategies in this book over the course of many years in order to enrich the reading experience in our content-area classes. They can be used in and between all subjects as a way to develop strong readers who can comprehend, think about, and discuss what they read.

MIND stands for Meaningful Interdisciplinary Nonfiction Dialogue. Throughout this book, we introduce strategies that are "MINDful" as part of quality instruction for adolescents. The explanation behind the acronym is the essence of this book:

- ■ *M: Meaningful study* in the content areas is what helps students make deep connections. Educators must go beyond the textbook to create meaningful reading experiences and not just reading assignments.

- ■ *I: Interdisciplinary study* is when students develop a depth of understanding that can be transferred among subject areas. Focus questions that guide their analysis and evaluation of content are an essential tool for fostering this type of instruction.

- ■ *N: Nonfiction* is the type of text that most students will interact with in the real world. Integrating nonfiction (particularly narrative nonfiction) in a classroom under the guidance of a teacher who has content-area expertise gives students an enriched reading experience. Content-area teachers need to be teachers of reading, too.

- ■ *D: Dialogue* about text is an ongoing and culminating experience for students. Understanding multiple perspectives and engaging in fluid discussion about text builds comprehension and analytical skills. This also supports adolescents as they develop a sense of empathy for others in and out of the classroom.

5

Literature Versus Nonfiction

Nonfiction is an integral part of the Common Core State Standards across content areas. While some people see informational text as purely textbook reading, the CCSS expand the definition of this to many more types of nonfiction text. There has been much controversy about who is going to teach all this nonfiction. Many English Language Arts (ELA) teachers are terrified that they are going to lose the time to teach classics and other great literature due to this emphasis on nonfiction. In fact, the Common Core calls for seniors in high school to be reading an average split of 70 percent nonfiction and 30 percent fiction. On October 17, 2012, the *Washington Post* reported on this conflict and referred to it as the "Fiction vs. Nonfiction Smackdown." We have witnessed our share of disagreement about this, and we feel that there can be a common ground.

It seems that the media and others have become fixated on these numbers, but they may be overlooking the not-so-fine print. The CCSS Introduction clearly states that "Fulfilling the Standards for 6–12 ELA requires much greater attention to a specific category of informational text—literary nonfiction—than has been traditional. Because the ELA classroom must focus on literature (stories, drama, and poetry) as well as literary nonfiction, a great deal of informational reading in grades 6–12 must take place in other classes" (corestandards.org, 2010, Shared responsibility for students' literacy development, para. 4).

In fact, that footnote serves to further support the fact that the bulk of nonfiction reading will *not* be taking place in the ELA classroom, as it states, "The percentages on the table reflect the sum of student reading, not just reading in ELA settings. Teachers of senior English classes, for example, are not required to devote 70 percent of reading to informational texts. Rather, 70 percent of student reading across the grade should be informational" (p. 5).

The writers of the CCSS have spoken out against this backlash. David Coleman, president of College Board, wrote a letter to *The New York Times* in response to an op-ed by Sara Mosle in which she claimed, "What schools really need isn't more nonfiction but better nonfiction, especially that which provides good models for student writing." Coleman said that the writers of the CCSS see fiction as having a "central role" but he noted that, "The change the standards make to the grades 6–12 ELA classroom is to invite more literary nonfiction as defined in the standards, including essays, narrative nonfiction and other literary writing to a wide audience that makes an argument or conveys information. Our country's founding documents and the great conversation they inspired are offered as explicit models for high-quality literary nonfiction for the ELA classroom."

We believe that the MIND format of reading helps alleviate fears for all teachers and meets the goals of the CCSS. There is a wealth of fantastic narrative nonfiction being published every day. The MIND strategy supports the reading of engaging, well-written, thought-provoking, complex nonfiction. The powerful and complex primary source documents that the CCSS cite in its reading lists can be incorporated to enrich any unit, but most content-area teachers (especially in social studies) have copious resources and experience with teaching primary sources.

Stretching Beyond the Textbook © 2014 by Lauren K. Francese and Rebecca H. Marsick, Scholastic Teaching Resources

Reading nonfiction is not a replacement for reading fiction. In order for students to be well-rounded, thoughtful readers, they need a strong dose of both. The larger issue is that most content-area teachers are not trained to be reading teachers and are worried about increasing an already packed curriculum, getting through the content, and all the other responsibilities that come with being a teacher. What new demands and challenges will they face if teaching reading is added to the list? It is a reasonable question that school administrators and teachers are going to have to answer together.

Our hope is that the strategies in this book help solve that problem. By using them, you will be teaching your students how to read the nonfiction that you are going to incorporate into your curriculum. But the most important element to keep in mind is that you will be adding engaging nonfiction texts that will help support and strengthen the curriculum and content that you are already teaching. This is not adding more work, but rather making the work that you currently do more meaningful and pleasurable for both you and your students.

Who We Are: A Summary in Two Voices

Lauren: As a social studies teacher, I am responsible for not only delivering content but also making sure that my students understand it on a level so that they can synthesize, evaluate, and transfer information from one historical event to the next. No longer is social studies about memorizing dates and facts. The focus now is more on understanding WHY certain events occurred and gaining insight into the decisions, people, and events that changed the course of history. Students must be able to see how these ideas have influenced and shaped our current world, which means they need a deep understanding of content and the ability to use effective strategies while reading.

Rebecca: Lauren and I would often engage in discussions about how to get students more interested and motivated in our classrooms. The buzzwords emerging at the time we began working together seemed to be "real world" writing, thinking, and problem solving. So, how do we bring "real world" or "authentic" learning into our classrooms?

We both came to teaching with graduate degrees that had a strong emphasis in literacy. The foundation of our collaborative relationship is based upon the philosophy that *all teachers are teachers of reading*. Together, we began to look for ways to establish more effective reading routines in our classrooms. As this process was unfolding, the Common Core State Standards were released. We found that our model supported the skills that are outlined in the new standards. From this new partnership, a collaborative effort was born: a nonfiction reading experience for content-area classrooms.

Rebecca: As an English Language Arts teacher, I have been using literature circles for years and was embarking on a new type of group reading: book clubs. Since we shared rooms with world language teachers in our building,

Stretching Beyond the Textbook © 2014 by Lauren K. Francese and Rebecca H. Marsick, Scholastic Teaching Resources

Lauren would come through the squeaky dividing door every plan period and sit and work in my room.

Lauren: *Without having a wall to divide us, Rebecca's room naturally became a collaborative environment. We spent many hours discussing students and their progress. As the year wore on, so did our frustrations with the way our students were developing as readers. I was frustrated with my students' struggles with nonfiction reading. I noticed an overall reluctance to read, and when they finally dug in, their comprehension was only surface level.*

Rebecca*: I also found that many students were not reading outside of school at all, and I attributed this to the fact that they hadn't been connected with the right books. The few who chose to read were not exploring different genres, preferring to stick with fantasy and realistic fiction.*

For more than five years, we have worked together to teach strategies in both of our classrooms that benefit students as readers and writers. As a team, we have read countless books to find the ones that are engaging as well as appropriate for diverse reading levels within the framework of the district curriculum. In addition, we have collaborated to create lessons that benefit our students as readers, not just as social studies or ELA students. For example, after we both modeled metacognitive reading strategies in our classrooms, a student raised his hand and commented, "I've never read like this before." What has emerged in our classrooms as a result of this kind of teaching is an environment where deep thinking and questioning while reading is the norm.

Our model of MINDful reading is what we want to share with you. As you explore this book, think about the experiences you want to create for your students. How will you nurture the adolescent readers in your classroom this school year and in the years to come?

Stretching Beyond the Textbook © 2014 by Lauren K. Francese and Rebecca H. Marsick, Scholastic Teaching Resources

CHAPTER 1

The Reading Experience in the Content-Area Classroom

Every reader finds himself. The writer's work is merely a kind of optical instrument that makes it possible for the reader to discern what, without this book, he would perhaps never have seen in himself.

—Marcel Proust

Picture this: You hand out an article on the effects of dropping the atomic bomb on Hiroshima to your class. As a teacher of social studies, you're excited to discuss the significance of this event with them. Not wanting your students to simply memorize the facts, you plan to make them think about the United States' actions during World War II and, finally, to have a culminating conversation about who really wins and loses in a war.

Your directions are clear: "As you read this article, use your highlighter to annotate, thinking about the focus question: *Who really wins and loses in war?*" The class gets to work. Other than a few comments to one another along the way, students appear to be engrossed in the short article. You see a great deal of highlighting (and make a mental note: students need a mini-lesson on restraint in highlighting) and a few margin notes (and make a mental note: students need additional mini-lessons on how to annotate), but for the most part, you believe your students comprehend the reading.

9

Soon you're ready to discuss the article. You write the focus question on the board and, below it, an additional one: *Do you think Japanese feelings about the United States' actions in Hiroshima are similar to the way Americans feel about the Nazis' actions across Europe? Why or why not? Use evidence from the article, as well as the notes from the unit, to support your points.*

You look around for a volunteer to begin the discussion. No one volunteers. Crickets. You reread the questions on the board and ask if anyone needs clarification. Nothing. Finally, Jeff raises his hand and asks, "Did the bomb explode when it hit the ground?" You stare at him . . . and then notice three other hands shoot up to ask follow-up questions. After weeks of studying this subject, the only topic they want to discuss is the explosion?

You close the door after the last student has left the classroom and reflect on what you could have done better that day. What was missing in your teaching today? Your students had been studying World War II for weeks and had been assessed, both formally and informally, so the background knowledge box should have been checked. The article you gave them today was at an appropriate reading level, so why, when you asked them to pull it all together, were they unable to synthesize the information, or even, on a more basic level, understand the facts?

As teachers of adolescents, we are caught between two worlds: elementary school where students are learning how to be independent, and the adult world where people are independent readers. In elementary school, students are learning to read, but in the secondary school setting, they are *reading to learn*. Is this really fair? Have we, as secondary teachers, given our students the tools and strategies that they need in order to comprehend a text—especially a nonfiction text, of which there are a multitude of subgenres? Or do we expect that because students have left elementary school, they should be able to read anything deemed at an instructional or independent reading level? Not only do we expect students to be able to comprehend nonfiction texts, we also ask them to apply this new information to various subject areas. We cannot forget the cognitive requirements necessary to perform in this capacity. The newness of these skills can be debilitating for an adolescent without a classroom model that scaffolds, encourages, and ultimately, nurtures a still developing reader.

We are content-area teachers; we also need to be teachers of reading. This is not a new assertion, and teaching students how to read in a content-area classroom is becoming more and more essential with the emergence of the Common Core State Standards. We believe that the MIND model of reading in content-area classrooms is a powerful instructional tool that will not only produce stronger readers but also readers who are also able to engage in deep reading and to create new ways of looking at the content. In essence, we believe that the MIND model of reading is a powerful way to develop strong readers, thinkers, and collaborators.

To Comprehend or Not to Comprehend

Over the years, reading instruction has taken a serious hit in America—a situation that educator and author Kelly Gallagher (2009) cleverly refers to as "readicide." He defines readicide as, *"Noun: the systematic killing of the love of reading, often exacerbated by the inane, mind-numbing practices found in schools."* The practices he is most referring to are the ever-increasing amounts of test prep that students are forced to endure in order to pass standardized tests. Yet the more we prepare students for these tests, the weaker their reading skills are becoming. This is mostly due to the fact that test prep is not *authentic* reading. However, this is what today's students associate with reading. It is no wonder, then, that we are living in a country where:

- The percentage of students ages 12–18 who read books not required for work or school dropped from 59 percent in 1992 to 52 percent in 2002.

- The percentage of 17-year-olds who say they never or hardly ever read surged from 9 percent in 1984 to 19 percent in 2004. This is a sharp contrast to the number of 13-year-olds asked the same question. That percentage went from 8 percent in 1984 to 13 percent in 2004.

- The average time spent reading in 2006 for 15–24-year-olds was 7 minutes during the week and 10 minutes on weekends or holidays.

- The percentage of 12th graders reading at or above the proficient level declined from 40 percent in 1992 to 35 percent in 2005 (compiled from National Endowment for the Arts 2007 study, *To Read or Not to Read*, p. 7–20).

These numbers are frightening considering these students will one day enter the workforce. When employers were asked what basic skills they considered as "very important," 63 percent said reading comprehension. These same employers rated 38 percent of high school graduates as being deficient in reading comprehension for the jobs they were applying for.

This study also found that people who were proficient readers were more likely to volunteer (57 percent versus 18 percent of below-basic readers); vote (84 percent versus 53 percent below-basic readers); find employment (78 percent versus 45 percent below-basic readers); and stay out of prison (3 percent versus 40 percent below-basic readers). These statistics make clear that being a lifelong, proficient reader directly correlates with being a strong citizen. If we are aiming to teach students to think globally, respect other cultures, and make positive contributions to society, then we must also teach them to read, and not just the passages on a test.

Gallagher also argues that one of the main ways we are committing readicide is that American schools have not given students "the opportunity to develop recreational reading habits; the focus has been on preparing students for exams, and as such, students are overdosing on a steady diet of academic texts. High-interest reading materials have been set aside" (pp. 79–80). Oftentimes, content-area teachers do not put high-interest texts into students' hands, especially not high-interest nonfiction. Instead, we hand them textbooks that have watered-down information, just the bare

11

facts. We do not ask them to identify the author's purpose in writing the book because the purpose is already clear in each chapter title and subheading. Teachers don't explore the concept of author's craft while using textbooks because the writing in these books is formulaic. There is nothing wrong with using textbooks, but the reading experience should be enriched through the use of nonfiction books. Consider the textbook to be your curricular anchor, but use rich nonfiction texts to deepen your students' understanding of the content.

Before we start thinking about how to engage our students in reading, we must first look at our own engagement in reading. Do you read textbooks for fun? Do you read for fun? When is the last time you read a really gripping nonfiction book? If it wasn't recently, then check out the literature cited on pages 114–115. Today, there are wonderful nonfiction texts being written, in every genre and on every topic imaginable. Many of these texts are appropriate for middle school and high school readers. But, in order to help your students become lifelong readers, you must be one as well. So pick up a book and begin the journey.

A Brief History of MINDful Reading

Before continuing with how we have developed the MIND method of reading for the content areas, we would be remiss if we failed to mention its forefather: the literature circle. Developed in the early 1980s, the literature circle started with the idea of bringing educators together to talk about professional texts and then evolved into a strategy used with students in the classroom. Currently, millions of students participate in literature circles, predominantly in ELA classes.

Literature circles have become a strategy for teaching reading comprehension and helping students interact with text (Daniels, May 2002, p. 7). In *Moving Forward With Literature Circles*, the authors write that, "in literature circles, we can see the process of comprehension unfold . . . discussion helps strong readers gain more control over comprehension strategies . . . it allows struggling readers to see comprehension modeled and practice it" (Day, Spiegel, McLellan, & Brown, p. 18). However, the literature circle model has rarely left the ELA classroom. Educator and professor Chris O'Brien (2007) suggests that literature circles should be renamed "reading circles" because the former term discourages the use of nonfiction texts as part of the strategy. As a consequence, other content-area teachers historically have not seen this strategy as designed for their classrooms and haven't used literature circles as a way of teaching comprehension in their subject areas. One reason for this may be that literature circles are seen as a way of improving comprehension, not content knowledge. However, we believe that adapting the model for the content areas can improve comprehension as well as content knowledge.

In 2006, Cindy O'Donnell-Allen published *The Book Club Companion*, which advocated for a more pleasurable, real-world approach to teaching texts in small groups. This new model met our students' needs better than the more structured approach that literature circles offered. Book clubs have existed in the adult world for centuries, but it has only been in the past few decades that they have become a part of mainstream American culture. In "The Book Club Phenomena," Katie Wu (2011), claims that in 2003 "a Google search for 'book club' returned 424,000 hits; now it returns 40 million." Our students often talk about watching parents buried in a book because their "book club meets in two days and they have to finish!" In fact, one of our students read *The Other Wes Moore: One Name, Two Fates* by Wes Moore because her mother read it for her book club and was so enthusiastic that she persuaded her daughter to read it. This student then went on to recommend it to us with as much passion as her mother must have shown, and it has since made the book list for our unit on American identity.

In 1996, a revolution was born when Oprah Winfrey introduced book clubs as a regular part of her talk show. Since then, she has recommended 70 books, all of which have set sales records. Her Web site features an entire section on which books to read, stories from successful book clubs, and even an article titled "How to Read a Hard Book." Oprah recognizes that even adults are continuously growing as readers and need reading strategies along the way.

There is no specific study that shows that the book club phenomenon has created a nation of readers, but it does appear to have helped. In *Literature Circles: Voice and Choice in Book Clubs & Reading Groups*, Harvey Daniels cites evidence that book clubs are on the rise. He claims that in 1990 there were about 50,000 book clubs in the United States, a number that doubled by 2000. Wu cites the National Endowment for the Arts (NEA) *Reading on the Rise* survey that states "that for the first time since 1982, the number of U.S. adults reading literary material had risen from 46.7 percent in 2002 to 50.2 percent in 2008. In all, 16.6 million more adults are reading today than at the beginning of the decade." In the real world, book clubs have helped create a growing number of adult readers by providing both recommendations for high-quality texts as well as a social environment for discussing and enjoying reading.

Both literature circles and book clubs consist of small groups of readers who meet regularly to discuss one text or multiple texts, but there are several differences between the two. Literature circles are focused on a specific task for a short period of time. Book clubs offer students the opportunity to continue reading together as a group. The other major difference is the flexibility book clubs offer. In literature circles, readers have role sheets that drive discussion, and students rotate through these roles at each meeting. In book clubs, students can use a wider range of tools to respond to a text without following specific roles. The book club navigates collaboratively and circularly through different levels of critical thinking, and readers work together to infer, synthesize, and analyze nonfiction text (O'Donnell-Allen, 2006, p. 13).

However, we still struggled with how to make the discussions during book clubs meaningful without having to structure them because we wanted to:

- Give more ownership to students by having them learn through dialogue with one another

- Have students connect what they were learning in various texts to content in the classroom

- Provide more explicit strategies for reading comprehension

- Differentiate instruction

■ Meet the skill-based standards presented in the CCSS

From these earlier models and through our own classroom experiences, professional study, and questioning, the MINDful Reading method was born.

MINDful Reading: An Instructional Strategy for the 21st Century

The MINDful reading experience refers to the reading of a whole book or selected excerpts of a text with a curricular/content-area focus grounded in literacy instruction and student dialogue.

MIND is an instructional strategy wherein groups of three to four readers meet regularly to discuss a text. The idea behind MINDful reading is that students are motivated because they are in charge. Adolescence is a time when students are seeking independence, but they still need support to facilitate that independence. MINDful reading helps foster this by allowing students to take ownership of their learning. The level of independence varies because MINDful reading can have many different formats depending on the skills and strategies you want to use to support your students, not just on how you want to deliver content.

The MINDful reading experience is when students:

» *Read a whole book or selected excerpts of a text*

» *Explore a curricular or content-area focus in depth*

» *Practice essential literacy skills*

» *Engage in thoughtful dialogue with their peers*

THE ELEMENTS OF MINDFUL READING

A MIND reading unit consists of several elements, which shape the experience for students. There is flexibility in the planning of these units, but the key components will support a grounded and scaffolded instructional model for both you and your students.

Texts: In any given unit, you may choose to read one book with the class (a whole-class text) or give students a list of books to choose from (student-selected texts) that revolve around a unit topic or theme. MINDful reading is about engaging in an authentic conversation about the text, not one that is dictated by the role the reader has been given for a specific passage. This reflects O'Donnell-Allen's assertion that books discussed in book clubs can be selected by students from a teacher-approved list (2006, pp. 2–3).

Choice: While it is not always appropriate or possible to have students choose suitable texts, we have found that if students have choice through the book-selection process, they are more likely to be engaged in their reading. There is a sense of responsibility and independence that comes with this choice. Adolescent readers can be expected to choose the "right" text; when presented with options, they will challenge themselves. When choice was introduced to MINDful reading in Lauren's 8th-grade social studies classes, students chose to read extensive adult biographies about Nelson Mandela and Martin Luther King, Jr., as well as *Two Sides of the*

14

Moon by Dave Scott and Alexei Leonov, a dual autobiography about the space race. Reluctant readers have devoured detailed photographic texts such as *Team Moon* by Catherine Thimmesh.

Schedule: Groups meet in class two or three times per week for 15 minutes each, with one additional 30-minute reading period per week. You provide a meeting schedule, but students often determine their own reading schedule for the group and hold one other accountable for coming prepared to meetings throughout the week. It is important that students know when their book club is going to meet and that the schedule remains consistent.

Organizers: Students independently complete reading organizers and focus-question activities throughout the reading process in order to demonstrate comprehension and to promote discussion. These discussions are entirely led by students but monitored and facilitated by the classroom teacher. Through this, you can determine areas of strength and weakness and implement specific reading-strategy lessons for groups or the whole class as needed.

Discussion Ideas: Students come to their MIND group meetings with discussion ideas that they have generated based on what they were thinking, questioning, or wondering as they read.

Strategies: The strategies needed for comprehending nonfiction are different from the ones students use to comprehend fiction. Employing strategies specific to understanding text structures, text features, and the role of multiple perspectives allows students to learn about the content on a much more independent level. MINDful reading is instructional while giving students a sense of independence.

Whole-Class Dialogue: The culmination of each MINDful reading experience is a whole-class dialogue based on the Socratic method. Students meet for a dialogue about the topic, using a combination of teacher- and student-generated questions. This final conversation allows students to synthesize both new and old information in evaluating the topic or theme of the unit.

The Rationale for Whole-Class Dialogue

Using a culminating dialogue is an important component of the reading experience for both the students and the teacher. For the student, this dialogue is where a synthesis and evaluation of the content occurs. For the teacher, this dialogue is where you assess student knowledge and skills. However, it is important to note that this dialogue is not designed to facilitate debate. Debate is an instructional strategy used predominately in social studies classes and tends to focus on two sides of an issue. The purpose of the MINDful reading experience is to get students thinking about multiple perspectives and drawing unique conclusions based on their reading. Adolescents are great at debating (and arguing), but encouraging students to engage in a dialogue that moves thoughtfully and fluidly brings them to new understandings about the content. It also teaches them how to productively collaborate and have a shared experience without perceptions of winning and losing.

Stretching Beyond the Textbook © 2014 by Lauren K. Francese and Rebecca H. Marsick, Scholastic Teaching Resources

Dialogue Versus Debate

	DIALOGUE	DEBATE
Fosters critical-thinking skills through the process of fluid discussion	X	
Requires students to use textual evidence to support ideas	X	X
Includes a formal process with opening/closing statements, rebuttals, and specific roles		X
Involves a whole-class meeting with opportunities for students to participate in discussion about a text	X	
Provides an opportunity for adolescents to give feedback to one another about collaboration skills in "real time"	X	
Requires planning and preparation	X	X
Revolves thinking around thematic questions as opposed to a specific content-oriented topic	X	

How MINDful Reading Experiences Can Support and Enhance Any Content Area

All content-area teachers have a unique opportunity when planning a MINDful reading experience: *variety*. Content-based curriculum can be organized thematically, and reading can be integrated in ways that enrich these existing units. For example, when teaching a unit on the space race, a social studies teacher could teach the content and then offer a MINDful reading experience where students evaluate the question: *Is competition a good or a bad thing?* In groups, students would explore this question through different perspectives, like those of women, astronauts, scientists, other nations, and the general public. The variety of books on these topics provide real-world

MINDful reading can be used in the content areas for the following purposes:

- » Developing nonfiction reading skills
- » Providing a collaborative reading experience that is both instructional and independent
- » Helping adolescent readers explore, question, and discuss topics beyond textbook, periodical, and primary-source material
- » Deepening understanding of content beyond the facts

16

understanding of the events and people involved, not just the facts and dates. Students can truly explore their own questions and interests with a group of peers and use texts to bring their personal perspectives to class discussion. At the culmination of a MINDful reading experience, an amazing transformation takes place in the classroom: Students think more deeply about a topic. They begin to question, explore, and analyze through a dialogue that incorporates different perspectives.

Harvey Daniels (May 2002) also reported that "the whole literature circle phenomenon has been pretty much driven by fiction" (p. 7), and he noted that nonfiction text could (and should) be used when implementing collaborative reading experiences in the classroom. He even stated that there is an "urgency" to begin using nonfiction text because of the increasing amount of nonfiction reading on standardized tests (p. 7). Daniels also explained that using nonfiction is challenging because there are many different text structures and genres within it. This is only further evidence that content-area teachers need to use their background as content-area experts to help students navigate the selection of text, as well as the understanding of that text.

Harvey Daniels recommends that all teachers use nonfiction text with the following "ingredients"

> "content that is important or engaging
> people we can care about
> a narrative structure or chronological line
> places we can visualize
> danger, conflicts, risks, or choices
> value, moral, ethical, or political dimensions
> some ideas that reasonable people can debate, dispute, or disagree about" (p. 11).

It is important to acknowledge that the MIND model should not be used with textbooks or other reference sources. These types of texts give overviews of topics and should only be used for background information, clarification, or reference during a MINDful reading experience. Appropriate book selection is an important component of the implementation of MINDful reading, and there is no shortage of appropriate, compelling, and engaging texts on a variety of topics.

Common Core State Standards and MINDful Reading

The CCSS state, "The Standards define what all students are expected to know and be able to do, not how teachers should teach" (corestandards.org, 2010, What is not covered by the Standards, para. 1). As classroom teachers, we find this statement to be incredibly freeing, and it is worth repeating at the beginning of any meeting regarding the Common Core. The CCSS do give flexibility to teachers, a flexibility that has allowed us to develop the MIND strategy for reading. Since literacy in social studies and science are incorporated into the standards, we can teach important literacy skills with engaging content. The CCSS provide teachers with guidelines for student outcomes. If we embrace the standards as a way to guide our instruction, we will be strengthening our teaching and supporting students through more rigorous reading, writing, and thinking.

In implementing the standards, content-area teachers will be expected to start integrating nonfiction reading—articles, books, op-eds, historical documents—and soon. The CCSS have two sets of standards, one for ELA and the other for the content areas of history/social studies, science, and technical subjects. The CCSS state that, "This division reflects the unique, time-honored place of ELA teachers in developing students' literacy skills while at the same time recognizing that teachers in other areas must have a role in this development as well" (corestandards.org, 2010, Shared responsibility for students' literacy development, para. 1).

In 2009, the National Assessment of Educational Progress (NAEP) published a framework advocating the increasing use of informational text as students progress through school. The Grades K–12 Literacy in Social Studies/History Standards "follows NAEP's lead in balancing the reading of literature with the reading of informational texts" (corestandards.org/ELA-Literacy/ introduction/key-design-consideration, Shared responsibility for students' literacy development, para. 4). The standards, created as a backwards-design approach, look ultimately at skills students need to be successful in college and careers. They define a "college and career ready student" as one who can:

> ### CCSS: Grades 6–12 Literacy in History/Social Studies, Science, and Technical Subjects
>
> *In order to maintain consistency, the breakdown of skills in the content areas and ELA are the same:*
>
> » *Key Ideas and Details*
> » *Craft and Structure*
> » *Integration of Knowledge and Key Ideas*
> » *Range of Reading and Level of Text Complexity*

- ■ "readily undertake the close, attentive reading that is at the heart of understanding and enjoying complex works of literature"

- ■ "perform the critical reading necessary to pick carefully through the staggering amount of information available today in print and digitally"

- ■ "actively seek the wide, deep, and thoughtful engagement with high-quality literary and informational texts that builds knowledge, enlarges experience, and broadens worldviews"

- ■ "reflexively demonstrate the cogent reasoning and use of evidence that is essential to both private deliberation and responsible citizenship in a democratic republic" (p. 3)

The MIND strategy of teaching reading is grounded in the principle that we want all students to develop a love of reading that will lead them to be deep thinkers who can evaluate and question what they read. If students have these critical-thinking skills, they will be more likely to be stronger citizens of the world, dedicated to thinking about the decisions that they make and understanding the actions and decisions of others. Engaging students with powerful nonfiction texts, and the dialogue that comes with that engagement, is one of the most important paths to take in this endeavor.

THE COMMON CORE STANDARDS MADE (SOMEWHAT) SIMPLE

The CCSS are not a curriculum. They are expectations for the skills students need to be college and career ready. This short comparison chart will help clarify the two:

COMMON CORE STATE STANDARDS	CURRICULUM
Sets high expectations for college and career readiness.	Sets high expectations for instruction and content.
Paces skills for students in specific grade ranges for reading, writing, speaking, and listening.	Paces the progression of the curriculum with student development and interest at its heart.
Supports and informs skill-based instructional design.	Creates opportunities for differentiated instruction and leaves room for teacher flexibility and choice.
Offers skill-based standards only; engaging instruction is up to the teacher.	Offers a rich and dynamic experience for students.
Provides teachers with clear guidelines that lead to consistent skill-based instruction for all students at a subject or grade level on a national level.	Provides teachers with clear guidelines that lead to a consistency for students in the subject, grade level, and community.

A Preview of MINDful Reading at Work in the Classroom

Succeeding chapters are dedicated to providing guidance, materials, and examples of MIND models for the content areas. There are also ideas for the development of nonfiction reading strategies as needed by specific students and teachers, but here is a general sequence for how the process works:

- The teacher selects either a whole-class text or generates a book list on a specific topic or theme for student-selected texts.

- The teacher delivers a book talk to generate excitement and interest in the whole-class book or the books on the list for student-selected texts. When presenting multiple books, the teacher shares the reading challenges that each book may present: writing style, length, perspective, and topic.

- Students select their level of challenge. For a whole-class text, the challenge level relates to the activities they will participate in during the reading process. For student-selected texts, students choose the book they are interested in reading.

- The teacher organizes groups based on either the level of challenge students have selected for a whole-class text or the individual books students have chosen for a student-selected text. Students meet with their assigned MIND group and plan a reading schedule based on a calendar provided by the teacher.

- Students read and prepare their assigned materials for each MIND meeting.

- Students meet with their groups two or three times per week for about 15 minutes each. Groups guide their own discussion using the materials provided. The teacher monitors and facilitates, as needed.

19

- Once students complete their book, they prepare questions for a whole-class dialogue. They also prepare evidence from their text in response to the topic or focus questions.

- The whole class participates in a dialogue in which students use the text to present their own questions and respond to the questions of others.

- Students complete an individual reflection concerning their reading process, new content knowledge, thinking, and collaborative experience.

This process can be modified to meet the diverse needs of students with a range of interests and reading abilities. The benefit of MINDful reading is that teachers can target specific content or skill-based goals throughout the process to meet the needs of the individual as well as groups of students. It is important to remember that this is a collaborative experience for the students and the teacher. The process is about exploration, engagement, and deep thinking. MINDful reading should be an activity that both students and teachers look forward to as a means of discussion and thinking about content-related topics.

Here's an example from a student who had built his academic identity around the idea that he hated to read. For a MINDful reading experience in social studies, knowing that his progress was being monitored by his teacher and peers, he reluctantly read a book of his own choosing. Here's what he wrote about *No Choirboy* by Susan Kuklin at the end of the year:

I [Mike] am a reader. Three months ago I was not. What changed such an important thing, but the thing itself. Let me explane, I am big, I am strong, I am brave, I am unbroken. I am . . . I was never scared. The book Know Choirboy did something that years of impossible tricks and accidents never did. No Choirboy scared me. I don't like being scared. I was never scared but this book took me somewhere I wish I could forget. This book talks about how kids, some inicent were sentenced to life in prison. That could be me. I good truly but the people I'm friends with, the people who enjoy the same activities I do. Well they are not. These kids where the same as me. I noticed myself relating to every person in one way or another and it scared me. Though it also taght me that people even in jail (for life or shorter) are people that injoy wrighting and reading, or just shooting ho[o]ps. They [criminals] are people, the[y] are human, the[y] are not worthless.

• • • • •

Establishing a focused and productive instructional method for incorporating nonfiction in a content-area classroom, or among teachers on an interdisciplinary team, is very powerful. As students begin to understand how to engage thoughtfully and deeply in their reading, they will begin to make connections between their own lives and the content within the curriculum.

20

Stretching Beyond the Textbook © 2014 by Lauren K. Francese and Rebecca H. Marsick, Scholastic Teaching Resources

CHAPTER 2

Planning a MINDful Reading Experience

> *Make it a rule to never give a child a book that you would not read yourself.*
>
> —George Bernard Shaw

The process of reading a nonfiction text with a content-area teacher enriches students' learning experiences. For example, in Lauren's opening unit on World War II, students begin the year reading *Hiroshima*, by John Hersey. Tough book? You bet, and for a variety of reasons, too. But there are significant benefits to introducing a complex text into a content-area classroom. Here is a 13-year-old student's reflection on reading *Hiroshima* as a whole-class text in social studies:

All throughout the book the six main characters vividly described their memories of the atomic bomb, including gory "images" of the living and dead. On page ninety a kid simply explains the order of events of her encounter with the A-bomb. The . . . story lacks detail and she tells the story (as Hersey says) almost "gaily." This proves that children are golden and can find the good in evil, whereas adults have trouble classifying it. Many optimists may say that it is a wonderful thing that only kids can find good in tragedy. But to a thirteen year old girl who is becoming a woman it isn't, because I still want to be innocent and see all the good in the world. But I can't, and I won't because I am growing up, and that was my personal rude awakening from the book Hiroshima.

Applying the appropriate planning, implementation, and reflection strategies will lead your students—and you—to thinking about content in new ways.

21

Stretching Beyond the Textbook © 2014 by Lauren K. Francese and Rebecca H. Marsick, Scholastic Teaching Resources

Initial Planning

In your initial planning, think about how you want to incorporate nonfiction text. Do you want the entire class reading the same book? Do you want to provide several texts for students to choose from? This is up to you and is highly dependent on the topic. Lauren chose to read *Hiroshima* as a whole-class text because of two factors: the level of difficulty in comprehending the multiple perspectives and her science teacher colleague's interest in using elements of the book to discuss atomic energy. This was an opportunity to create an interdisciplinary unit, and they went with it. Could they have offered a variety of texts about the dropping of the atomic bomb? Of course, but grounding their classes in one book gave both teachers the ability to focus on specific concepts and ideas in their content areas.

In contrast, when Lauren began her Space Race unit, she offered a variety of texts so her students could examine the history of those events from multiple perspectives. The science teacher taught a unit on forces in motion in conjunction with this but did not explicitly teach from the same texts that Lauren offered to her students. The most important things to identify in the planning process are the content of the unit, the skills you want students to learn, and the needs and interests of individual students.

PLANNING WITH THE CCSS

The CCSS outline four major areas to address for reading: Key Ideas and Details, Craft and Structure, Integration of Knowledge and Ideas, and Range of Reading and Level of Text Complexity. As the chart on the next page shows, it is clear that many of the skills for college and career readiness are embedded in our existing units. Key Ideas and Details and Craft and Structure are addressed in more detail in Chapter 4, where we share some reading lessons and strategies. Range of Reading and Level of Text Complexity are the focus of this chapter since they are very important (and widely misunderstood) elements of nonfiction reading.

TEXT COMPLEXITY

The CCSS have increased the level of text complexity that is required at each grade level. No longer is it enough to just hand the most advanced readers challenging texts; we must make sure that complex texts are given to all readers. In "What Reading Does for the Mind," Cunningham and Stanovich note that, "Ability is not the only variable that counts in the development of intellectual functioning. Those who read a lot will enhance their verbal intelligence; that is, reading will make them smarter" (p. 147).

Identifying appropriate texts for the classroom can be a challenge, and the CCSS provide guidelines for selecting texts. The components in the diagram at right are discussed on pages 23 and 24.

Aligning the Standards With Appropriate Reading Strategies in Grades 6–12

KEY IDEAS AND DETAILS What content can the student discover?	• Citing evidence • Analyzing a source • Identifying central ideas • Summarizing • Detailing steps in a process or sequence of events • Evaluating and explaining using text
CRAFT AND STRUCTURE How and why is an author presenting the information or ideas?	• Meaning of words and their use in a text • Analyzing text structure • Evaluating an author's purpose and/or perspective • Assessing an author's claims, reasoning, and evidence
INTEGRATION OF KNOWLEDGE AND KEY IDEAS What insights can be gained from reviewing a diversity of textual and visual information on a topic?	• Using visual information to gain insight (charts, graphs, and so on) • Distinguishing fact, opinion, and reasoned judgment • Analyzing primary and secondary sources on the same topic • Evaluating an author's claims using other information • Integrating sources and evaluating multiple perspectives • Noting discrepancies between sources
RANGE OF READING AND LEVEL OF TEXT COMPLEXITY Am I engaged in an appropriately challenging reading experience?	The CCSS outline text complexity bands in which students at each grade level should demonstrate proficiency.

Qualitative: Levels of meaning, structure, language conventionality/clarity, and knowledge demands are the important elements here. When planning, ask yourself the following questions: *Will my students be able to interact with this text? What might they need in order to interact with this text?*

Quantitative: This relates to the readability (level of vocabulary) of the text, which is commonly measured in Lexile levels. Use Lexile levels as a *tool*, and not as a *rule* when selecting books. Exposure to challenging vocabulary in context and with a content-area expert enhances the opportunities for pushing young readers to interact with challenging books. Students' vocabulary cannot be expanded unless they are exposed to new and advanced vocabulary. A list of books that we have used and their corresponding Lexile ranges appears on pages 117–118.

23

The chart below shows the association between text complexity bands in the CCSS and Lexile ranges.

TEXT COMPLEXITY GRADE BANDS IN CCSS	OLD LEXILE RANGES	LEXILE RANGES ALIGNED TO CCR EXPECTATIONS
K–1	N/A	N/A
2–3	450–725	450–790
4–5	645–845	770–980
6–8	860–1010	955–1155
9–10	960–1115	1080–1305
11–CCR	1070–1220	1215–1355

Source: corestandards.org/assets/Appendix_A.pdf

Reader and Task: Reader variables (motivation, knowledge, and experiences) and task variables (purpose, the complexity generated by the task assigned, and the questions posed) contribute to the reading experience. This is where teachers thoughtfully plan reading experiences considering student interests and differentiate to foster enhanced engagement. (Source: corestandards.org/ELA-Literacy/standard-10-range-quality-complexity/measuring-text-complexity-three-factors)

These guidelines are very brief, however, and don't explain a few important nuances, so we've included a fourth component in the text complexity triangle as one of the main factors for evaluating readability of a text:

Rigor: Simply stated, the Common Core is recommending that you triangulate the information you have available about your students as readers to create a rigorous experience for them in your classroom. Rigor is not about the quantity of work that you assign, but rather the quality. As Strong, Silver, and Perini note in *Teaching What Matters Most: Standards and Strategies for Raising Student Achievement,* rigor fosters students' ability to understand content that is "complex, ambiguous, provocative, and personally or emotionally challenging." At the core of planning with qualitative, quantitative, and reader/task measures lies the rigorous reading (and learning) experience. Rigor is about presenting students with opportunities to be challenged.

Think about this: You assign a textbook-reading activity with follow-up readings that include primary document excerpts. You create comprehension questions and discussion questions or use the ones in the textbook. This is typically how content is presented to adolescents in the classroom, and it is still okay to use this as part of your instruction. But ask yourself this question: *What is challenging about this to my students?* Is it challenging because there are ten questions to answer? Is it challenging because the primary document is handwritten? Is it challenging because of the volume of text and the attention it requires? While these elements might make it challenging for a student to answer the questions, the amount of time that a task takes does not equate to the level of cognitive challenge.

Now shift your thinking: You provide students with a nonfiction book that is rich and complex. Students read the entire book (or excerpts) and consider a focus question that requires them to think about deeper connections between the text, the world, and themselves. You might even provide supplemental primary sources, even in the original handwriting. Students must integrate all this new information to address the focus question. Now ask yourself the same question: *What is challenging about this*

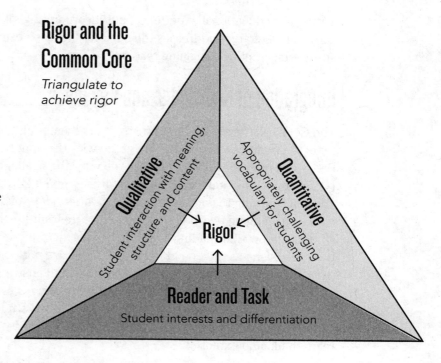

Rigor and the Common Core

Triangulate to achieve rigor

Qualitative
Student interaction with meaning, structure, and content

Quantitative
Appropriately challenging vocabulary for students

Rigor

Reader and Task
Student interests and differentiation

to my students? Here, the challenge lies with the individual student. Does the student struggle to empathize and connect to the world outside his or her community? Does the student feel challenged because he or she needs to read critically, follow a sequence of events, and persist while reading? Is it challenging for the student to understand how the primary source and nonfiction text share similar ideologies? MINDful reading creates a rigorous experience for students through the use of complex text, dialogue, and a unique experience for each reader in your classroom.

Range of Reading

The MIND strategy was specifically designed for use with complex texts. In recent years, school textbooks in the content areas have been designed to incorporate reading strategies and colorful images and graphics. This has been a positive addition for content-area instruction and certainly makes texts more accessible for students. But exposure to nonfiction books and articles is important for students as well. Authentic reading experiences beyond a textbook will help students identify complex nonfiction when they see it in the world after secondary education. When it comes to nonfiction, students need to explore a variety of genres with a content-area teacher.

We have found that many students who struggle to remain engaged in fiction can find their niche in nonfiction. Knowing that a story, experience, or account is real presents a different level of engagement. A student who wants to be an engineer often sees no reason to be motivated to read *The Catcher in the Rye* or *A Portrait of the Artist as a Young Man*, but provide a nonfiction text such as *Paperboy: Confessions of a Future Engineer* and that student is suddenly a reader! Rich literature should always be part of a student's educational experience, but incorporating meaningful and engaging nonfiction across subject areas addresses the need for more exposure to nonfiction and may also absorb reluctant or struggling readers.

Integration of Knowledge and Key Ideas

The Common Core states that "instructional materials should also offer advanced texts to provide students at every grade with the opportunity to read texts beyond their current grade level to prepare them for the challenges of more complex text" (Coleman & Pimental, p. 3). As you start designing MIND units for your classroom, you will continue to add more texts at a variety of levels. Asking students to persist with a challenging text helps them explore their interests. It is important to let students know that reading a hard book is okay. Tell them that the reading experience is not the same as the one in ELA class. They are not reading to understand in tremendous detail; they are reading to try to find answers to the focus questions you have assigned. Knowing every detail of the book is never a requirement, but thinking about the text is. This is also why it is essential that students have *both* types of experiences. We need to encourage students to pick texts that will challenge them to read, think, and explore.

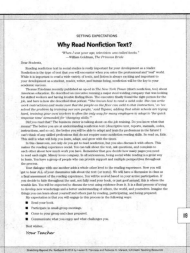

Teacher Tip: Set Expectations

To provide a context for students about why they will be engaging in this reading experience, we send them a letter that sets expectations (see page 119 for a sample).

Designing a MIND Unit

The fundamental rules for planning depend upon how your district or school chooses to allocate time. Here is a list of questions to ask yourself, school administrators, and/or colleagues before you begin planning:

- Do you have to stay on a strict curricular schedule?

- Do you have flexibility to spend time on the curriculum as you see fit?

- Are there certain areas of your curriculum that you want to explore in depth with your students?

- What texts are available to you?

- What supplemental resources are available to you?

- How much planning time do you have?

- How long are your class periods?

26

- How often do you meet with your students?
- How comfortable are you with student-led reading groups?
- What are your personal interests? What are your students' interests?
- Are you in a collaborative setting?

All of these are important questions to answer before you can begin planning any MIND unit. But do not let any of your answers keep you from trying the process. Don't be afraid to start small. We have accumulated the strategies and resources in this book over years of planning and across a wide range of units. Pick and choose what works for you. The only hard and fast rule is that you are comfortable with the material and some ambiguity!

As you begin your planning, there are multiple steps to consider. Each of the steps outlined below will support the development of a unit that will allow both you and your students to feel successful.

STEP 1: *Define your goals and objectives.*

As you begin to design your MIND unit, think about your specific goals for your content area. Your curriculum outlines the content and skills that you will teach during the school year. Begin by reflecting on the unit you are teaching and how it can be enhanced with the incorporation of multiple texts for a MINDful reading experience. Here's an example that includes a focus question for Step 2:

Unit: Studying the Bill of Rights

GOAL: *By the end of the unit, I want my students to think critically about the rights of American citizens and discuss how citizens' rights are jeopardized in America today.*

OBJECTIVES:

» *Students will identify the individual liberties outlined in the U.S. Constitution.*

» *Students will discuss how individual liberties have been jeopardized.*

» *Students will analyze potential solutions/resolutions for protecting individual liberties in America today.*

FOCUS QUESTION:

Why is it important to establish and protect the individual liberties of citizens?

After writing your objectives, determine which ones will be addressed through direct instruction and which will be addressed through the texts in MIND groups. In the above example, the first two objectives will be addressed through direct instruction. For the third objective, the MINDful reading experience will help students arrive at higher-level thinking by requiring them to read a text and think critically about the specific issues it addresses. The result will be an understanding of the Bill of Rights *and* a deep

27

connection to how and why the rights of the individual citizen are so important for a thriving democracy.

STEP 2: *Develop focus questions.*

Once you've outlined curricular goals and objectives, and you are clear about where and how the MIND groups will support them, you can begin developing your focus questions. Before you hand out a text, decide why students will be reading it. The purpose should not be just to teach the facts for a topic in your content area. Instead, you want to come up with one or more focus questions that will lead beyond your current unit, something that can be applied to future units so students see the connection between the ideas presented throughout the year. Focus questions aim at delving deep into the curriculum and should be open-ended. In addition, you should never be looking for one specific response. The responses to a focus question should change and evolve throughout the unit, and even the year, and allow students to deepen their knowledge and thinking. These questions give students a focus for both the unit and their reading. As students read, they should be constantly looking for examples that answer the focus questions. Most important, these questions give groups a foundation for meaningful discussion.

Sample Revisions of Content-Based Questions to Create Focus Questions

- » **Content Question:** How is the French Revolution a model of revolutionary activity?
- » **Focus Question:** How do revolutions emerge and what gives them purpose?
- » **Content Question:** Were colonized people the victims of conquest or the beneficiaries of it?
- » **Focus Question:** How has imperialism shaped the world?

We developed two focus questions in our ELA and social studies classes for *Hiroshima.* Our first question was, *What do multiple perspectives tell us about events in history?* The study of history often involves looking at multiple perspectives in order to understand decisions that were made and the impact they had on others. *Hiroshima* is written from six different perspectives in order to give a more complete picture of what happened in the days leading up to and after the bombing. The focus question about perspective works for the MIND experience because it fulfills the following criteria:

- ■ It may be applied to multiple units.
- ■ It is appropriate and engaging for the age group.
- ■ It solicits diverse opinions.
- ■ It fosters meaningful discussion.
- ■ It creates opportunities for deep thinking.
- ■ It is open-ended.

28

Our second focus question was, *How do people respond to a tragedy or disaster?* We chose this question because the social studies department had set unit goals to make connections between the tragedy in Hiroshima and 9/11. This is not a question that can be answered by looking at the facts in the book but rather through a deeper exploration of the topic.

Well-developed focus questions can take a content-oriented approach and add rigor in new ways. As students begin to see that their thinking about the focus question is valued, they will become motivated to dive deeper into a complex text. Have you ever had a really thoughtful and productive discussion with students after reading a textbook chapter? It's pretty rare. There's typically not enough evidence (rich text) in a textbook for students to sink their teeth into. The 13-year-old who said reading *Hiroshima* was her "rude awakening" about growing up probably would not have recognized that kind of connection without a complex text and a focus question that required deep thinking.

COMMON FOCUS QUESTIONS

Using complex texts encourages students to develop their own responses and thoughts about the focus questions based on what they are reading. This creates unique and varied perspectives in the classroom. When developing focus questions, you have a lot of flexibility. The expectations in the curriculum can often be confining; be brave and think about focus questions in this manner:

■ What questions will help students connect history to their own lives?

   Possible Focus Questions:

   - *Is it okay to break the rules sometimes?*
   - *Do young people have the power to inspire change?*

■ What questions will help students develop understanding and empathy for others?

   Possible Focus Questions:

   - *How does scientific development impact human beings?*
   - *What is the role of justice in America?*

■ What questions will foster a whole-class discussion on the content as it relates to global citizenship?

   Possible Focus Questions:

   - *What are the rights and responsibilities of citizens of the world?*
   - *How am I connected to others around the world?*

Questions like these allow students to make deeper connections while reading. As the MIND groups meet, students develop their understanding of the questions and begin to think critically. One of the challenges in the content-area classroom is to avoid having students see history as "stuff that happened back then" or "stuff that is happening over there." Framing focus questions that ask students to bring their own life experiences together with a topic fosters a more productive and thoughtful experience in the classroom.

29

STEP 3: *Select a whole-class text or a variety of texts for students to choose from.*

Whole-Class Texts: The most important reason for planning a reading experience for a whole-class text is that it furthers student engagement in a curricular topic. Here are other considerations for choosing a whole-class text:

- It establishes a common foundation of knowledge among your students.
- It will encourage students to ask questions about the topic.
- It will engage students so that they want to know more about the content.
- It can be differentiated for a variety of readers. (For more on differentiation, see Chapter 3.)
- *You like the book!*

Student-Selected Texts: There are often many engaging books written on a specific topic. These books can provide multiple perspectives and/or a variety of reading levels. If this is the case, you can strengthen your curriculum by offering a variety of texts for a particular topic in order to provide more choices for students.

VARIATIONS OF TEXT

At the beginning of this chapter, we discussed Lexile levels for specific books as one measure of text complexity. These levels have a time and a place in reading instruction to inform book choices, but they should not restrict you from choosing an engaging text. Think about a time you picked up a book you were interested in and realized it was hard to read. Did you persevere because you liked the topic? Did you search for a different text on that topic that was more manageable? Did you ask for help or seek out more background information? These are skills that adults develop, and strategies often vary based on our individual dispositions and preferences. While students should not be reading texts in which they do not understand a single word, a little challenge and heightened interest can transform a non-reader or reluctant reader into an engaged one. Remember, you have the ability to support individual students who may need additional help with a text. In addition, students are reading in groups during MIND units, so they have the added benefit of discussion with their peers instead of only having themselves to rely upon. In the content areas, interest should be the primary motivator in selecting texts.

For example, in Lauren's class, a group of girls of mixed reading abilities selected *Promised the Moon*, by Stephanie Nolen, a book that she presented as a challenge, for the Space Race MIND unit. This group became so engrossed in the story of women who successfully tested as astronauts only to be rejected for a moon mission by all levels of government that it soon became impossible to tell the difference in the girls' reading abilities. The best part: in the culminating dialogue, they all tried to convince the rest of the class that both John Glenn and John F. Kennedy were given too much credit in the other books and asked their classmates to think about the opportunities denied to these women in the name of competition with the Soviet Union. It didn't matter if this group didn't understand every nuance of the text. What did matter was that they were

30

so engaged in the *content* that they were willing to challenge themselves. In the process, they not only became stronger readers, but they also were able to think deeply about an important historical and social issue.

With content-area texts, vocabulary building can be supported by the teacher who is the expert in each content area. For example, *Team Moon* (which looks almost like a children's picture book) has a higher Lexile level (1060L) than *To Kill a Mockingbird* (870L) because *Team Moon* contains scientific and technical terms. Instead of eliminating a challenging text as an option, offer it as a selection and support students who choose it with strategies for breaking down the technical language and vocabulary. In book talks, students discuss the level of challenge of the book's vocabulary, the amount of time a book takes to read, and the difficulty of the content. Student interest should drive text selection.

Although we always give students a 24-hour grace period with a book, they rarely change even after taking the book home. Students commit to their books and want to persevere. One student noted after reading Nelson Mandela's biography—a long and challenging read—during the last unit of the year, "We talked about Mandela in class, and I really wanted to know more about him."

Content-Area Reading and Levels

Reading specialists often identify three levels when assessing reading abilities:

- Independent
- Instructional
- Frustration

The content-area reading experience can occur at all three levels for students, but intervention is required if a student is at the frustration level. For a whole-class text, it's important to focus on how the common text will meet the instructional needs of the class and be accessible to all students. This requires differentiated instruction, strategies for which are discussed in Chapter 3. For student-selected texts, the books should fall at different levels; however, you must be on the lookout for students who seem to be at the frustration level. When students enter this realm, they are most likely to attribute their frustration to reading in general, which is a slippery slope. If you witness this, step in and talk through the situation with the student. More than likely, this will mean finding a new book (and most likely a change to a different group since this is a student-selected text) for the student. You will need to be an understanding and a supportive coach as each student finds his or her way through a text. Everyone will have different needs throughout the process.

CHOICE AND FLEXIBILITY

Choice generates students' enthusiasm, and assigning a text can diminish the excitement surrounding the process. However, you may find that you need to assign the books for each small group to read. For example, if your class contains many students who are receiving reading support, specialized instruction, or accommodations, you may have no

Stretching Beyond the Textbook © 2014 by Lauren K. Francese and Rebecca H. Marsick, Scholastic Teaching Resources

other choice. In these instances, you need to work with the reading teacher or special education teacher to make reasonable choices about specific texts.

You might also decide to assign texts because they are connected to a specific project that will follow the small-group reading. The following example from a science class makes a good case for this approach. The teacher planned a unit on bridges and wanted students to work in groups to do the following:

- Design a bridge to meet the needs of a specific community.
- Explore the types of bridges and determine the best option for the community.
- Read about that specific type of bridge and where it has been used.

In this example, students chose which type of bridge they wanted to study and were assigned a book that directly met the needs of the project. Student interest was still driving the project, but the primary objective of understanding bridge design and solving a problem became the central focus. As a result, students used nonfiction text in a meaningful way. The final products were richer because students defended their choice of bridge design with historical examples, engineering details, and deeper description—all gleaned from their reading.

STEP 4: *Design a prereading assessment.*

To initiate a MIND unit, it is often necessary to administer preassessments. It can be helpful to present students with a short reading assessment to help them reflect on their own reading process. There are two types of preassessments: multiple choice and highlighting key points and/or reflection. In implementing these assessments, you can help students develop an understanding of how well they read to learn.

When designing a preassessment, do not hesitate to make it challenging. This assessment shouldn't be counted as a grade because students have had no prior instruction in this area. Choose a grade-level text for the assessment, which will serve as a baseline and will help you group students appropriately. Then select a chapter or a section of a text and create questions. As you develop questions, think about having at least one of each of the following types of questions:

- *Observation:* Students need to look at captions, title, and text to respond.
- *Literal:* The answer can be found "right there" in the text.
- *Author's Purpose/Perspective*: Students have to think about what the author means.
- *Evidence*: Students have to determine where they would find evidence to support an idea or position.
- *Search*: Students need to search through a large section of text to determine a sequence, multiple perspectives, or meaning.
- *Highlighting*: Students make marks in the text to show evidence for a term, idea, or theme.

Pairs of preassessments—multiple choice and highlighting—for a biography unit on

Lincoln and a World War II unit appear below. Students had a choice of several books on Lincoln, but we wanted them to understand themselves as readers before making a choice. In addition, we were trying to determine which reading strategies we would need to address in our social studies and ELA classes.

Since *Hiroshima* was a whole-class text, the preassessment gave us information about how students would read the book. Based upon students' reading comprehension levels, we determined that some would read the entire book and others would read sections of it.

In both of these examples the multiple-choice questions are the more traditional questions in the assessment. The highlighting preassessments are based on new tests that are more oriented toward the CCSS. They require students to independently cite specific information when making inferences or to support a claim. It is critical that students are able to understand and respond to both types of questions. The more flexible they can be in their critical thinking and problem solving, the better.

Sample Preassessments for the Lincoln Unit

Multiple choice: This prereading assessment is based on Chapter 1 of *Lincoln: A Photobiography* by Russell Freedman. Students need to read and take notes on the first chapter. The goal here is not to have them remember what they read, but rather to have them engage with the text in order to show a deep level of understanding and thinking. Students complete the assessment "open book."

Highlighting: This assessment is more subjective for scoring purposes, but asking students for a specific number of examples to highlight helps us collect relevant data.

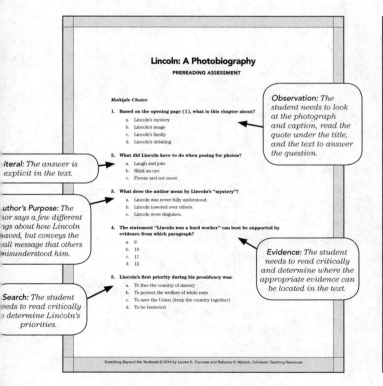

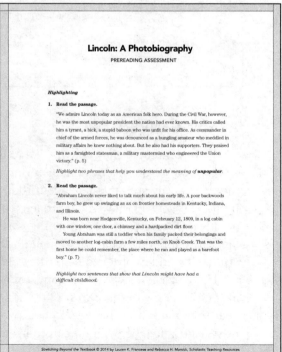

Sample Preassessments for the World War II Unit

Multiple choice: This prereading assessment is based on Chapter 1 of *Hiroshima*. Students need to read the chapter and make notes. Then they complete the assessment using the text and their notes.

Highlighting: For this assessment, students are asked to evaluate the perspectives of individual characters in the text, an important element when engaging in deep reading of *Hiroshima*.

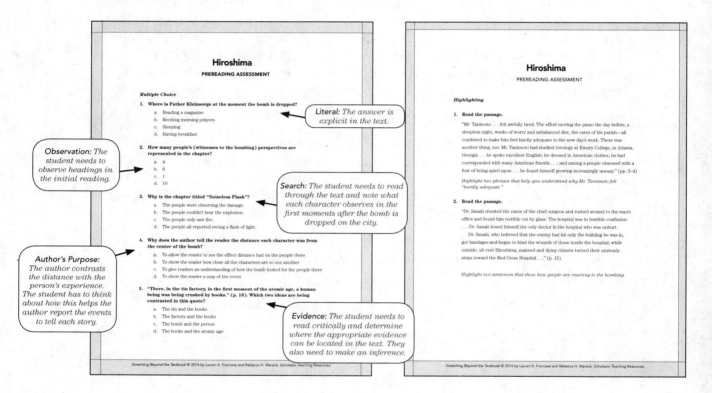

READING INVENTORIES

At the beginning of the year, we like to get a sense of how students feel about themselves as readers. We do this by administering a reading inventory, another type of preassessment. The way students feel about their own strengths and weaknesses as readers can influence the way they will approach a text. Sometimes students are very aware of their abilities. Other times they think they are stronger readers than they really are, or they lack the confidence that they should have. In any case, it's important to know where students stand in order to help them choose appropriate books.

There are a few ways to administer a reading inventory. Students should complete one at the beginning of the year for baseline data and be reevaluated throughout the school year to monitor any changes in their perceptions. The reading inventory shown on the next page is for the beginning of the year.

34

Directions: Categorize yourself based on your feelings and history regarding reading.

	LEVEL 3 (I'm not an eager reader.)	**LEVEL 2** (I'm eager enough.)	**LEVEL 1** (Can I read more than one book at a time?)
READING	I feel okay about my reading abilities, but I sometimes find it hard to focus on my reading.	I feel good about my reading abilities and understand what I am reading most of the time.	I feel that I am an excellent reader, and I comprehend what I am reading whenever I read.
AMBITION	In the last year, I didn't read everything assigned in class.	In the last year, I read everything that was assigned.	In the last year, I read all the time, far and above what was assigned in class.
FEELINGS ABOUT SUBJECT AREAS	I do not generally like this subject: *Science Social Studies Math Language Arts*	I am looking forward to learning a new curriculum in: *Science Social Studies Math Language Arts*	I am looking to be challenged further in: *Science Social Studies Math Language Arts*
TIME MANAGEMENT/ LONG-TERM ASSIGNMENTS	I sometimes have trouble getting my work in on time.	I usually get my work in on time.	I always get my work in on time and often start assignments early.
GOALS FOR THIS UNIT	I don't plan on working harder than usual.	I plan on putting in some more effort so that I can read a more challenging book.	I really want to read a challenging book and am willing to make other sacrifices so that I can do this to the best of my ability.

STEP 5: *Form groups and plan for differentiation.*

Preassessment data and inventories will help you plan for differentiated instruction as you move forward to implementing a unit.

GROUPING

As a result of providing students with choice, you will inevitably have small groups with a wide variety of reading levels. Regardless of the levels of readers in each grouping, it's important for students to know that they are grouped based on their interests. Emphasize that the goals for the group will be to discuss, question, and think

A reading inventory to administer throughout the year appears on page 120.

Stretching Beyond the Textbook © 2014 by Lauren K. Francese and Rebecca H. Marsick, Scholastic Teaching Resources

about what they are reading. The group determines how they will complete the reading on time and will facilitate their own discussion based on focus questions provided by you.

> ### Teacher Tip
> We make a point of telling students that it doesn't help to choose books based on what their friends are choosing. One of the reasons we give them choices is so we can create groups based on interest, but we also look at the potential dynamics of each group. The group has to work together to discuss the text, and these dynamics play a large role in this process. And remember, as the teacher, you always reserve the right to change groups that are not working.

ASSIGNING READING

For the whole-class text, you assign the pages or chapters to be read based on the needs of your students. Make it a rule to *never* give students less than two nights for an assigned reading. We use this as a way of teaching students to manage their time. At the beginning of the year, if you assign 30 pages over three nights, several students will inevitably complain that they had too much reading. This gives you a wonderful opportunity to talk about planning. Was 10 pages a night over three days too much? Was 15 pages a night over two nights a lot? The conversation often ends with the student confessing that he or she had waited until the final night to read all 30 pages. Those of us who work with adolescents in the classroom every day know that there need to be natural consequences for poor time management, otherwise students will not develop this important skill.

If you can, provide some reading time in class, too. At the beginning of the year with the first MIND unit, we set aside reading time in class so we can monitor students, answer questions, and identify those who may be struggling with the text. As the year goes on, students become increasingly independent, but being generous with some class reading time is a good way for you to convey the importance of deep reading.

SELECT ORGANIZERS FOR READING AND ANNOTATING.

Based on the skills/strategies you are teaching, choose an appropriate organizer for students to complete while they are reading. To develop an organizer, start with text structure. For example, *Hiroshima* clearly has a structured sequence of events, and students must follow different people in the book through their experiences before, during, and after the bombing. The important thing is to keep the organizer simple. Having students record four or five important things that happen in a chapter is sufficient. Remember: The reading experience should not be about remembering every fact or detail. It should be about leading students to think about the focus question. Information on the Description text structure shown on the next page and other text

structures appears on pages 122–123. Sample organizers for a variety of text structures appear on pages 124–132.

Description

The author provides detailed information about a topic, concept, event, person, idea, or object by listing characteristics, features, facts, and details. This includes language that is literal and/or figurative.

Words That Help You Recognize Description:

- » for example
- » such as
- » some characteristics are
- » look at
- » it is like _____
- » look closely, and you'll see . . .
- » it is as _____ as _____ (*makes a comparison*)

When annotating, students should give evidence for and reflect upon the focus questions. For example, have students read a section of text and chart the sequence of events on their organizer. In addition, they should be annotating the text for passages that help them understand, make them think about, or wonder about the focus questions. Students then bring both their organizers and annotations to their group meetings to help guide the discussion.

Overview of a MIND Meeting

When students arrive at their MIND meetings, they participate in a discussion that they lead themselves, but one that is structured around their organizers and annotations. Here's an overview of an effective MIND meeting:

- ■ Students have the book, reading organizer, and annotations with them.

- ■ At the beginning of class, students do a Write-to-Think activity. We like to start by writing a quote on the board. Students take a few moments to read it, think about it, and write a response. Samples appear on page 133.

- ■ Have students discuss their responses in groups. This is a good way to get them talking about the text. Saying, "Take out your reading organizer and talk about it" can be a total flop!

- ■ Then have students talk about the focus questions as they relate to the assigned reading.

- ■ Tell each group to select an idea they talked about, a quote they discussed, or something they are wondering about to share with the rest of the class.

- ■ End the MIND meeting by having each group share. Provide directions and materials for the next meeting.

Stretching Beyond the Textbook © 2014 by Lauren K. Francese and Rebecca H. Marsick, Scholastic Teaching Resources

- Set aside the first or last 15–20 minutes of class for MIND meetings. Don't drag them out. Keep the meetings short, interesting, and devoted to thinking about the focus question.

- We recommend having students meet twice a week. This allows them to have time to read between meetings, but not so much time that they lose momentum. Since the books are tied to your curriculum, this also allows you time for relevant teaching and activities that will enhance students' reading and understanding of the content. Below are sample calendars for two units.

Sample Book Unit Calendar
WHOLE-CLASS TEXT: *HIROSHIMA* BY JOHN HERSEY

DAY 1 Introduction to the atomic bomb: student notes	**DAY 2** Reading assessment (formative): Students read Chapter 1 and annotate. Language Arts class: Students take the 10-question assessment.	**DAY 3** Choosing a reading level and annotations modeling Language Arts class: Review reading assessment and re-annotate Chapter 1 as a whole class	**DAY 4** Group assignments Mini-lesson: Examining details in nonfiction text	**DAY 5** Reading time in class for Chapter 2 *Note*: No meetings for Chapter 1; it is done as a whole class. Mini-lessons for whole class or small groups as needed
DAY 6 Write-to-Think Book groups meet about Chapter 2	**DAY 7** Intro to 9/11 and class discussion	**DAY 8** Reading time in class for Chapter 3 Mini-lessons for whole class or small groups as needed	**DAY 9** Truman and the end of World War II— student notes	**DAY 10** Write-to-Think Book-group meetings for Chapter 3
DAY 11 Reading time in class for Chapter 4 Mini-lessons for whole class or small groups as needed	**DAY 12** Lesson on memorials— Hiroshima and Ground Zero	**DAY 13** Write-to-Think Book group meetings for Chapter 4	**DAY 14** Reading time in class for Chapter 5 Mini-lessons for whole class or small groups as needed	**DAY 15** Write-to-Think Book group meetings for Chapter 5
DAY 16 Work on Dialogue Preparation Sheets	**DAY 17** Seminar/ Dialogue Day	**DAY 18** Reflection writing in class	*Note*: On meeting days, you can plan mini-lessons or work in time for other topics (e.g., current events). We have also built in time for reading in class. This unit can be shortened if you have students do all their reading for homework.	

Sample Book Unit Calendar

STUDENT-SELECTED TEXTS: LINCOLN STUDY
Level 1: *Killing Lincoln* **by Bill O'Reilly (high)**
Level 2: *Lincoln: A Photobiography* **by Russell Freedman (middle)**
Level 3: *Abraham Lincoln* **by George Sullivan (low)**

DAY 1	DAY 2	DAY 3	DAY 4	DAY 5
Intro to Lincoln Primary document reading activity	Video: *Life and Times of Abraham Lincoln* (Delphi)	Book talks and selection	Slavery in America	Book assignments and groups
DAY 6	**DAY 7**	**DAY 8**	**DAY 9**	**DAY 10**
Write-to-Think: Document Group meetings Organizer: What Makes You Think That?	Reading time in class	The Gettysburg Address	Write-to-Think: Image Group meetings Organizer: What's Happening?	Reading time in class
DAY 11	**DAY 12**	**DAY 13**	**DAY 14**	**DAY 15**
Write-to-Think: Image Group meetings Organizer: What Makes You Think That?	Freeing of Slaves: Emancipation Proclamation	Reading time in class	Write-to-Think: Document Group meetings Organizer: What's the Big Deal?	Dialogue preparation in class
DAY 16	**DAY 17**	*Note:* This calendar gives you a snapshot of what can be going on in class throughout a book unit. Student organizers can be customized based on book selection or changed based on how you plan to present/discuss the content.		
Seminar/ Dialogue Day	Reflection: Lincoln remembered			

Supporting the Development of Lifelong Readers

Teachers often tell us, "Kids just don't read!" or "They're reading books in English class. They can't read in my class, too." Our response is not to make predictions that students will fail before giving the practice a try. We know students will walk in completely unprepared for class for a variety of reasons. One of the strengths of the MIND process is that a student who hasn't completed the reading assignment has to face his or her

Stretching Beyond the Textbook © 2014 by Lauren K. Francese and Rebecca H. Marsick, Scholastic Teaching Resources

classmates who have; however, the student can still be a part of the group and will benefit from hearing the discussion. Don't underestimate how beneficial listening to meaningful dialogue can be for a reluctant reader. Other students will model good work habits, use evidence to support their ideas, and demonstrate how they are learning through the process.

A student with significant attention and reading issues appeared disconnected throughout *Hiroshima* in the World War II unit, but in his final reflection, he shared this:

> *Another word to describe this book would be "recovery" since many of the Japanese people had to recover from this tragedy. "Weeds already hid the ashes, and wildflowers were in bloom among the city's bones." This I thought represented the Japanese people, and how there was still hope even though everything had been lost. The wildflowers refused to stop growing. Seeing the perspective of all these people that had suffered during the day we dropped the bomb made me feel empathy for them. It was not the civilians fault that the war started, but we drag them into the war, the day we decided to drop the bomb on Hiroshima. This had an impact of how I look at history and wondered maybe sometimes we are not always the good guys.*

Honestly, we know that you may be reluctant to incorporate reading experiences into the content areas, but think about it this way: There are students who really don't like to exercise. Do they still participate in physical education classes? Of course! Even if they lack athletic prowess, they benefit from practicing skills, observing others, and learning about a healthy lifestyle. Reading is no different. It's okay for students to engage in the process in different ways. There will be a wide range of abilities, interests, and engagement throughout each unit and the school year. Accept that and move on to plan MIND units that will meet the needs of your students. One of the best things about teaching is when one of our reluctant students suddenly shows interest and demonstrates deep thinking.

No matter how much you differentiate or attempt to teach the strategies supporting the CCSS, students will not become better readers if they don't pick up a book and read. Kelly Gallagher (2004) emphasizes that students "must have interesting books to read." We argue that every student has his or her own idea of what interesting is. This is why student choice is so necessary. We provide models for whole-class texts and student-selected texts because both experiences are important to incorporate throughout the school year. Allowing students to select their own books is the most manageable way to provide choice, but as we discussed, it's not always feasible or suitable for some units. For whole-class texts, choice is offered through what students will do throughout the process of reading. Planning this can be more challenging, but it shows students that they can exercise some choice even when they are reading the same book as their peers.

40

The International Reading Association (IRA) proposes that adolescents should have:

> » Access to a variety and choice of texts
> » Instruction that "builds both skill and desire"
> » Teachers who can instruct based on the individual needs of students
> » Teachers who can assess reading skill development appropriately
> » Curriculum and instruction that explicitly teach strategies across content areas

As discussed in Chapter 1, student choice can sometimes make the difference between creating a reader and a student who is a reading bystander. We gave you a glimpse of this with Mike's statement on page 20. For us, one of the most incredible parts of reading Mike's reaction to *Hiroshima* was when he stated, *I [Mike] am a reader. Three months ago I was not. What changed such an important thing, but the thing itself.*

Not only did Mike acknowledge that there had been a shift in how he saw himself as a reader, but he also recognized that what created this shift was the act of reading itself. The experience opened Mike's mind to thinking that reading could be an exciting and thought-provoking experience. But more than this, he now understands that reading has *relevance* and *purpose* in his life and world. This only occurred because Mike was given the opportunity to choose a book that he was interested in reading.

● ● ● ● ●

At the start of a MIND unit, it may seem daunting to think about all the considerations for your students. As you bring your planning together, keep in mind that the more effective you become at planning and responding to students' needs, the more independent students will become as they read. Teaching students how to be successful readers of nonfiction is a marathon, not a sprint.

Stretching Beyond the Textbook © 2014 by Lauren K. Francese and Rebecca H. Marsick, Scholastic Teaching Resources

CHAPTER 3

Introducing and Managing MINDful Meetings

Until I feared I would lose it, I never loved to read. One does not love breathing.

—Harper Lee from To Kill a Mockingbird

One of the important decisions to make for a MIND unit is whether or not students will read a whole-class text or select a text from an approved list you've generated. If you choose to plan a unit with a whole-class text, you will need to place more focus on strategies for differentiating instruction during the unit. If you choose to plan a unit with student-selected texts, your focus will be on text complexity (range of reading levels) and the range of content. Either way, a MIND unit should provide choices and flexibility in order to motivate and engage students.

The Power of Choice

A resolution adopted and published by the International Reading Association in 1999 described adolescent literacy as "being just as important and requires just as much attention as that of beginning readers"—and this affirms our belief that content-area teachers must be reading teachers in their specific subject areas. This can be done without sacrificing the content-area focus that middle and high school teachers hold dear.

Adolescent literacy strategies need to revolve around motivating and building confidence. In Pitcher, Martinez, Dicembre, Fewster, and McCormick's (2001) analysis of struggling adolescent readers at a university reading clinic program, researchers tested and surveyed a group of struggling readers to make determinations about their needs for reading instruction. While several of these students were participating in a prescribed reading intervention program at school, testing showed that they were still having trouble with comprehension, most critically with nonfiction text. As the researchers noted, "Since most of the reading they will do during the rest of their schooling and in future employment will be in this type of text, instruction needs to focus on strategies for understanding its different types" (p. 643).

It was clear that the students in the study had faced challenges when reading in the content areas because there was little reading instruction in those classes. The students also reported that they were able to understand text better when they were offered choice (p. 643).

In many content-area classrooms, the majority of the reading is done with textbooks. This type of reading is not "real world," nor does it teach students how to access the rich nonfiction writing they will encounter as they mature. This discrepancy further supports the need for explicit reading comprehension instruction in the content areas, as well as the need for teachers to create opportunities for choice in selecting texts that will be accessible, interesting, and motivating for the adolescent reader.

In addition to a choice of reading material, adolescents also require a sense of independence during reading activities in the classroom. Parents and teachers alike know the challenges of working with adolescents. They are constantly seeking independence, and want to make their own choices for just about everything. This is an important consideration when looking at reading instruction for this age group. In 2002, Thompson conducted a study in a small high school to determine why so many students were not performing well on statewide reading assessments. The researchers used focus groups and questionnaires to assess student attitudes toward the Accelerated Reader (AR) program, which had been implemented in the school as a strategy for fostering growth in reading for many students. Students reported that the AR program made them less likely to want to read for pleasure outside of school and admitted that they often cheated on the prescribed AR assessments that were given in ELA classes. Students who participated in the study did not like being "forced" to read certain texts and never being given the choice to read about topics of interest to them (Thompson, Madhuri, & Taylor, p. 5). Choice must be a part of the reading experience for adolescents so they develop comprehension skills as well as the independence to read beyond the classroom.

SELECTING TEXTS

You must be wondering how you will read all these books in order to offer choice and conduct book talks on an array of texts in your class. The reality is that you do have to screen books to make sure they are appropriate for students. There is no way around this. The initial development of a book group experience does take time, but once it is in place, you can add or remove books easily based on student interest and enthusiasm. This is a flexible process for both you and your students. You may choose to offer three or four texts at first. Our Human Rights unit book choices include close to 20 books right now, but it has taken time!

Here are strategies for helping you select books:

■ If you are working in a collaborative team, split up the books. Two or three teachers can bring their classes together for book talks and share the books they have screened.

■ Ask colleagues in your school for book recommendations. You can incorporate these books into MIND units and even invite your colleagues to do a book talk for your class.

■ Ask students to screen some of the books. Avid readers often enjoy reading and critiquing a book. They will be very honest, too!

READING ABOUT MATURE TOPICS

Books can be safe places to explore the scary and dangerous things about the world. Where television can often put images into a student's head, a book allows the reader to create and envision the story in his or her own mind. Offering texts on a variety of topics can help students understand and connect with content in a meaningful way. Historical topics, memoirs, and other accounts of the real lives of human beings often depict pain, suffering, and inhumanity. The small-group book meetings and the culminating dialogue allow students to think about these potentially upsetting topics in a safe classroom environment, one in which they are engaged and thoughtful as they discover new things about the world.

Here is a reflection from a teacher about using mature content while teaching social studies:

My first year teaching, I planned what I thought was a stellar Civil Rights unit. I started the unit with some background on civil rights: Plessy v. Ferguson, civil rights amendments, the legacy of the Civil War and so on. As I introduced the modern movement, students watched a video clip about Emmett Till, the young African-American boy who was brutally murdered for allegedly speaking to a white woman. Part of the video clip showed his disfigured body in an open casket. Now, this is well-documented history and I had, of course, seen this footage before, but my students had not. They showed a whole range of emotions: sad, grossed out, and shocked, just to name a few.

I realized in a split second that I had not prepared them for this, and I'm not really sure I could have. As a new teacher, I kept wondering if I should have even addressed the topic in my class at all. But an amazing thing happened after students saw that video clip: they asked questions. I had already talked about the civil rights struggle prior to the modern movement, but now they were really listening. They wanted to understand why such inhumanity existed in America. From that moment, the unit took off. It became driven by student interest.

We tell this story because mature topics can often establish an interest, context, and motivation for learning. Let's face it—adolescents are fascinated by the inhumane and unjust. They are looking for meaning in the world as they try to sort out who they are and why the world works the way it does. Simply watching the news on television or

44

online is disturbing, and students wonder and question as a result of what they see. To then present them with any type of watered-down content is not only unfair, but it also is not teaching them to connect and engage with their community and the world. While we do not suggest seeking out books on disturbing topics, our experiences have shown us that there is a value in being open-minded about texts. Students who read Loung Ung's *First They Killed My Father* about the Cambodian genocide in the 1970s often report that they didn't even know anything bad happened there, and then they research the events independently. The reality of injustice and inhumanity can be eye-opening and motivating, and most of all, it can bring students to a new level of understanding and empathy for other human beings. This is how we create responsible and kind citizens.

Introducing Texts in a Book Talk

At the beginning of the MINDful reading experience, you (and possibly some of your colleagues) need to take some time to present the books to students. We like to set up the texts in the front of the room a few days before beginning the book talk, so students will see them, become interested, or even flip through a couple. On the day of book talks, have students get comfortable. It can be fun to leave the classroom and sit on the floor in the library or use an outdoor space. The change in setting can make things intriguing. Create and copy a book list to hand out to students. For each text, include the author, title, a brief description (from a bookstore Web site or the back cover of the book), and the number of pages. Students can make notes on this list throughout the book talk to help them remember the books that interest them.

Introduce the unit and focus questions, then explain how they connect to the themes or topics students are currently studying. Start your book talk with the shorter, more manageable texts and work your way up to the more challenging ones. Share the following highlights with the class during your book talk:

- *Title and author:* Share something unique or interesting about the author.

- *Brief summary of the book:* What or who is the book about?

- *Style of writing:* Is the book a narrative or an informational text? Is it a graphic novel?

- *Specifications:* How is the book organized? How many chapters does it have? How many pages does it have?

- *A teaser about what students might learn:* Reveal something fascinating about the story. Are there things in the book that might surprise students? Does the book appeal to a specific interest like justice, exploration, or innovation?

- *A quote or an excerpt:* Read part of the first chapter, or show an image from the text. These should be exciting and end with a cliffhanger, enticing students to want to read the book.

Teachers need to demonstrate their enthusiasm for reading in order to get our students to read. If there is a particular book you like and want to share your excitement, don't hold back. Just be careful—most of your students may choose the

45

same book due to your selling power. We have had to order many more copies of *Almost Astronauts* by Tanya Stone due to Lauren's passionate book talk about women during the Space Race!

The Book Selection Process for Students

There are a few ways to have students select books from the texts you've gathered. The first is the simple pencil-and-paper method. Have students write their first, second, and third choices on an index card or a sheet of paper. The second method is to use an online survey that students can complete in school or at home. Create a pull-down menu of the book choices so students can select which texts they would like to read. This helps to effectively organize students without creating a lot of paperwork. There are several Web-based survey creators that you can use, such as Google Docs, SurveyMonkey, and Zoomerang. Once students have completed the survey, you can organize and view their responses in a spreadsheet.

SUPPORTING GOOD CHOICES

The book talk should be an opportunity for students to ask questions. They will inevitably be watching to see which book will be "easy" or "just right" or "too hard." Try to avoid using that language when speaking with students. Remind them that being interested in a text is the most important part because it will make the experience enjoyable for them. We like to remind our students that a big part of their grade is engaging in thoughtful dialogue about the text, and if they are not reading a book they enjoy, the quality of their discussion can be impacted.

It is also important to let students know that if they choose the "wrong" text, they can change. However, you do not want to make this a routine part of the reading process, as it takes time and thought to create groups. One change can be made relatively easily, but multiple changes can lead to a big headache! Therefore, it is important to encourage students to read the first page or so if they are not sure that a book is right for them. In addition, after the first few weeks of school, we have a pretty good idea as to the individual reading levels of each student. We always reserve the right to ask students to challenge themselves more, especially if we see that they are consistently choosing books beneath their reading ability.

On the flip side, we also speak with students who choose a book that we think is too challenging. We approach this by stating that we are so pleased that they want to challenge themselves, but we are concerned that the text may be a little too difficult. We reiterate that they should enjoy the reading; if it is too difficult, they will become frustrated, and this is not productive for becoming a better reader. Sometimes, we will suggest that they try a challenging book when there is not a time constraint, such as over a vacation, instead of during a defined period of time with a group. Overall, students are receptive to concerns as long as they feel they are part of the process.

COMMUNICATION WITH PARENTS

It is important to include parents in the MINDful reading process because students will need to be reading some of their selected books at home. Here are some of the strategies to use for introducing parents to book choices:

- Put the books out at Parents' Night. Invite parents to flip through them and even read one themselves.

- Publish a book list in advance so parents can see the choices and discuss them with their children. You can also put the list on the school Web site or attach it to an email.

- Send a letter home describing the unit and the purpose for reading the texts. This is a good strategy if you choose to incorporate books with mature topics.

- Always give parents the opportunity to discuss a book selection with you if they are not initially comfortable with their child reading it.

The Dialogue

This "Socratic Seminar" style method is modeled on the teaching style of the famous Greek teacher and philosopher Socrates. Socrates believed that deep, inquiring discussion, leading to the "discovery" of answers, is a superior method of learning to traditional lecture models. Therefore, in a Socratic seminar, participants sit together to discuss and discover meaning in a work through the use of open-ended guiding questions and firm textual support. Book dialogues at the culmination of a MIND reading experience are based on this method.

Introducing MINDful Meetings to Students

Meetings should have clear and predictable expectations for students. Below are directions for students to use to guide their meetings. A reproducible of the directions also appears on page 134.

Throughout the coming weeks, you will be reading your book and coming to class prepared for a small-group discussion. The details below explain what you need to do.

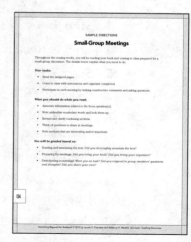

Your tasks:

- Read the assigned pages.

- Come to class with annotations and organizer completed.

- Participate in each meeting by making constructive comments and asking questions.

What you should do while you read:

- Annotate information related to the focus question(s).

- Note unfamiliar vocabulary words and look them up.

Stretching Beyond the Textbook © 2014 by Lauren K. Francese and Rebecca H. Marsick, Scholastic Teaching Resources

- Reread and clarify confusing sections.

- Think of questions to share at meetings.

- Note sections that are interesting and/or important.

You will be graded based on:

- Reading and annotating the text: *Did you thoroughly annotate the text?*

- Preparing for meetings: *Did you bring your book? Did you bring your organizer?*

- Participating in meetings: *Were you on task? Did you respond to group members' questions and thoughts? Did you share your own?*

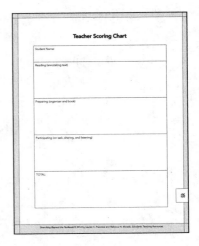

During each meeting period, as you work with different groups, you will be continually assessing students using the Teacher Scoring Chart. This chart is simple, so you can spend most of your time engaged with students and not bogged down with a lot of paperwork. A copy of the chart appears on page 135.

Organizing MIND Meetings

There are several ways to organize MIND meetings in your classroom, which are shown on the next pages. The most important thing is that the meetings should be no longer than 20 minutes. Older students may be able to sustain meetings for longer periods of time, but this is a good general rule.

As you begin, make sure that all students have a copy of the organizer you've selected for the text. You can do this as a hard copy or an online copy that students can access and type on. The method of delivering the organizer is based on your comfort level with technology as well as the accessibility of technology in your district or school.

Before giving any of these organizers to an individual or a group, always show a model lesson. For example, in a unit on Lincoln, we used a chapter from *In the Line of Fire,* by Judith St. George, to model the organizer we selected. The format for these lessons follows:

- *Step 1:* Give a short piece of the text and an organizer to each student.

- *Step 2:* Read through the directions and point out the features of the organizer.

- *Step 3:* Read aloud the text, stopping to explain your thinking. It is helpful to display a copy of the text on an interactive board or overhead projector.

- *Step 4:* Annotate the text based on your modeled thinking. Be specific about your responses to the ideas and questions on the organizer.

- *Step 5:* Complete the organizer using your annotations and input from the class.

- *Step 6:* Ask students to repeat this process with their assigned reading. This can be done individually or as a group discussion.

- *Step 7:* Ask individuals or groups to share their thinking process in a whole-class discussion. Encourage reflection about the reading and thinking process.

48

MIND Meeting Formats

The best thing about structuring meetings in the following ways is that students have a focus and a guide, but the discussion is motivated by their thinking and reactions to the text. This specifically targets the CCSS strands for Key Ideas and Details, which focus on using textual evidence to develop knowledge about the concept or idea, as opposed to using prior knowledge or opinion. Copies of the formats also appear on pages 136–138. Corresponding organizers appear on pages 124–132.

Meeting Format A

ORGANIZER: WHAT'S HAPPENING? (OR WHAT'S THE BIG DEAL?)

Directions for students:

- Discuss your organizers in your group. Focus specifically on what happened in this section of text and what connections to the focus question(s) you noticed.

- As a group, choose a quote that connects to the focus question(s). Be prepared to share it with the class.

TIPS FOR TEACHERS:

In this format, students have some open time for discussion before they go back to the text and choose a quote. Move around the room and monitor students as they select their quotes. Discuss with them the connection to the focus question(s). As a wrap-up for the meetings, have each group share a quote with the whole class.

What's Happening?

Directions: Complete the organizer by describing what you have read (summary) and how it connects to the essential question.

Essential/Focus Question: *What does it mean to be free?*

What's happening? Summarize important things in the text.	How does it connect to the essential question?
Man shoots Lincoln behind ear, jumps on stage, yells VA motto (confederate)	Man was free to walk in booth, shoot Lincoln. Where was L's protection?
Lincoln advised not to go in crowds, especially theater	Lincoln has freedom to ignore advisors - not like today
Lincoln gets hate mail, death threats, still goes out alone even at night	Does technology inhibit freedom? Was the gov't able to find who was sending threats? Did they even try?

What's The Big Deal?
Model: In the Line of Fire

Important Event READ WITH PURPOSE	Why is this a big deal? SHOW EVIDENCE	How does this help you answer the essential question? SHOW THINKING
Two of Lincoln's sons died.	This and leading the country during a civil war took a toll on Lincoln and he looked very old by age 56. (16)	Leadership- leaders have to persevere through their own personal struggles in addition to being a strong leader. This is a major challenge for an individual.
An assassin's bullet strikes Lincoln.	The president dies just as the civil war is ending. Andrew Johnson takes over. (30)	Freedom- Lincoln does not oversee Reconstruction and freed slaves and voting rights become Johnson's issues to face. The freedom of slaves and the establishment of their rights after the war might have looked very different.
Andrew Johnson takes over as President.	Johnson lost his temper and argued with people when they disagreed with him. As a result, he lost support of Congressional leaders. (31)	Leadership- Johnson was hot headed and failed at a harmonious reunion of the states. His leadership style and inability to work with others had an impact on the entire nation's ability to heal after the war.

49

Stretching Beyond the Textbook © 2014 by Lauren K. Francese and Rebecca H. Marsick, Scholastic Teaching Resources

Meeting Format B

ORGANIZER: WHY DO YOU THINK THAT? (OR WHAT DOES THE TEXT SAY?)

Directions for students:

- On your own, choose a quote from the text to share with your group. Be sure you can explain how it connects to the focus question(s).

- Share your quotes together. After someone shares a quote, everyone else should share their thoughts on how that quote relates to the focus questions. You can also ask one another questions about these quotes.

- At the end of the meeting, be prepared to share *three* interesting things you talked about during your meeting.

TIPS FOR TEACHERS:

In this format, students have to search the text more independently and bring their thoughts to the group in order to engage in discussion. This is a really good format for reluctant readers. As you monitor the group meetings, you will be able to see which students annotated and thought about the text as they read. Unprepared students will be shuffling around and might have a harder time making the connections, a signal to you to implement appropriate reading strategies for those students.

Why Do You Think That?

Directions: After reading the text, identify three important new understandings (things you have learned) from the book. Then explain why/how you arrived at that new learning.

New Learning/Understanding	Why do you think that? Use evidence (quotes) from the text.
Did Lincoln predict his death? Was he prophetic? more ahT	"Only weeks before he was shot... 'He was killed by an assassin!' " "Good night" "Good-bye" p 20
Were there hospitals? What kind of medical care was there? Would he have survived today?	"As the pres lay mortally wounded... carried across Tenth Street..." p 21
Robert felt guilty for the rest of his life - thinks if he was there, could have done something	"He could do nothing to help his father now..." p 22

Meeting Format C

ORGANIZER: WHAT MAKES YOU WONDER?

Directions for students:

- As a group, present questions about the text to one other. Are you wondering about an individual's motives or decision making? Have portions of the text confused you? Are there bigger questions about this topic that have come into your mind as you read the book?

- Share with your group and discuss everyone's ideas and thoughts.

- At the end of the meeting, be prepared to share *two* questions you discussed as a group.

TIPS FOR TEACHERS:

Questioning while engaging with a text can be a challenge for students. Sometimes, in groups with peers, students hesitate to ask questions because they worry about being judged. This format requires some patience and practice, especially with younger adolescents. It is especially compatible with memoirs, which typically feature a clear voice that encourages students to make personal connections and ask questions.

Meeting Format D

ORGANIZER: SEQUENCE OF EVENTS

Directions for students:

- Draw a picture related to an important part of the text.
- As a group, share your pictures and try to guess which portions of the text the artist is referring to.
- Once everyone has guessed (successfully or unsuccessfully), share the passage from the text that inspired the drawing.

TIPS FOR TEACHERS:

This is always a fun activity for a meeting. Most students enjoy drawing parts of the text, and the guessing game makes them really have to think about what they read. At the end of the period, you may choose to share a few drawings or have students post their drawings with the quote from the text written below it.

Meeting Format E

ORGANIZER: WHY DO YOU THINK THAT?

Directions for students:

- What surprised you while you were reading? Discuss parts of the text that made you think differently about the topic.
- As a group, identify *three* new understandings you have after reading. Be prepared to share with the whole class.

TIPS FOR TEACHERS:

This format is great for exploring informational texts in more depth. It will encourage students to point out when they've encountered new learning in the text. These new understandings can be a starting point for independent research and mini-lessons about topics that will engage students.

Meeting Format F

ORGANIZER: MULTIPLE PERSPECTIVES

Directions for students:

- Choose three people or groups from the text. Identify *each* different perspective.
- As a group, present each of the perspectives using evidence from your book.

TIPS FOR TEACHERS:

This is a great format for texts that include accounts from multiple people or that present diverse perspectives on a topic. Narrative nonfiction that describes the journey or experience of multiple people can also work well in this format.

51

Meeting Format G

ORGANIZER: EMPATHY

Directions for students:

- Try to empathize with, or "walk in the shoes" of, the people in your book. With your group, choose two people or groups and describe their situation.

- Then explain what it might be like to be in that situation. What might you be thinking about? How might you be feeling? What might you want/need/wish?

- Be prepared to share with the whole class.

TIPS FOR TEACHERS:

After reading a text, many students will reflect that they consider themselves lucky to have never experienced what the individuals or groups in their books have faced. That is not thinking deeply, that is feeling bad for someone. This puts students at a comfortable distance away from the text. Encourage them to explain what it might have been like to live like that person and to think deeply about the author's message. Was the story told just to make readers feel bad for them? Or does the author have a deeper message? This is where rich discussion develops.

Meeting Format H

ORGANIZER: WORDS FROM THE WISE

Directions for students:

- Identify important words or short phrases in the text.

- Explain the significance of these words, using evidence from the text.

- Share with your group.

- Write all your group's words on one sheet of paper and discuss connections between and among the words. What do these words have in common? What do they tell you about the topic or ideas presented in the text?

TIPS FOR TEACHERS:

Choosing just a few words encourages students to really look at the text in a different way. They have to reread text and pinpoint important words. This is crucial for developing as readers of nonfiction. You can pair this with a mini-lesson about bias and/or author's purpose. A whole-class discussion about why authors have chosen certain words or phases or a vocabulary review of important terms related to the topic can be naturally woven into the unit, and it is completely driven by students!

52

Working With Groups

The MIND reading experience gives you flexibility in the way students are grouped, both within the unit and on a day-to-day basis. If you choose to have students read different levels of books in order to meet the needs for a range of reading skills, you may find that the groups reading the most challenging texts are the most engaged, while the groups composed of struggling or reluctant readers have a harder time staying focused.

The first groups you should work with in a MINDful reading unit are the struggling or reluctant readers. Most of the time, the issue with these students is that they have trouble getting started. By working with them first, you can help guide them to focus. The graphic organizers give students both a task and a structured way to show their thinking about the reading. In addition, these students often do not complete their reading at home, so it helps to be able to sit and read a text with them to ensure their comprehension. This is part of the rationale for providing some time in school for independent reading. Usually, once students "get into" a book, they are more willing to read it at home.

On the other hand, it is important to not spend the majority of the class period working only with reluctant or struggling readers. With the incorporation of more complex texts, more struggling readers may emerge as they work to comprehend and think about their books. Therefore, students who are engaged in conversation are making progress on their own, but they might also need support. By joining these students in conversation, you have the ability to ask both clarifying and higher-level questions about the text. You can also gauge if individual students (or the group) would benefit from supplemental materials (e.g., articles, images, poems, primary sources, and so on) to enhance their thinking. We have also seen many strong readers who take over a group conversation. These students need to be taught how to take a turn, listen to others, and think about various perspectives.

For whole-class texts, feel free to mix the groups daily or weekly so that they are not always composed of the same students. It is important to remember that just because a student is having some reading issues does not mean that he or she is lacking important and thoughtful ideas to contribute. There are a variety of ways to mix groups:

- Have students choose cards from a deck and group students with like cards.

- Assign students random numbers and have like numbers work together.

- Use preassessment scores to create balanced groups based on the strengths and weaknesses of students.

Think about the dynamics of your class, and whether you will need to have more (or less) input in forming groups. You may find that as the year progresses you can give more control over grouping to students.

Since MINDful reading is about focusing on the same topic through texts, students can spend time in mixed-ability groups discussing a focus question. This allows all students to hear the ideas of the strongest and weakest readers. It elevates the thinking of students who think more literally and allows the strongest readers to see that others have great ideas too.

Stretching Beyond the Textbook © 2014 by Lauren K. Francese and Rebecca H. Marsick, Scholastic Teaching Resources

Differentiation

In *Integrating Differentiated Instruction and Understanding by Design*, Tomlinson and McTighe provide this definition for differentiated instruction:

Differentiated Instruction focuses on whom we teach, where we teach, and how we teach. Its primary goal is ensuring that teachers focus on processes and procedures that ensure effective learning for varied individuals . . . differentiation is predominantly (although not solely) an instructional design model (p. 3).

The implementation of differentiation in the classroom is often divided into three separate parts:

- ■ *Content*: the stuff in the book
- ■ *Process*: the manner in which a student reads the book
- ■ *Product*: the manner in which a student shares, presents, or shows engagement with the text

In our experience with (many) professional workshops, differentiation always seems to be presented as a simple method for meeting the needs of all students. But the reality is that differentiation is one of the most challenging strategies for teachers. And content-area teachers are faced with even more obstacles, depending on the curriculum's content, the lack of subject area-focused common assessments for reading and writing, and the needs of students.

What happens when you have a student reading and writing at a college level in your classroom? What if one of your students has an Individualized Education Plan (IEP) that mandates modified content or curriculum? How do you meet the needs of both types of students? Differentiation can easily boil down to creating multiple lesson plans for individuals or groups of students. Considering all of the demands that are part of teaching, this presents a whole new level of complexity and a delicate balance of equity and fairness in your classroom.

The MIND strategy is an experience in which book choices provide an angle for differentiation that can ease the burden since students self-select books based on interest and reading level. With a whole-class text, you can choose the areas for students to focus on while reading the text. With student-selected texts, you can provide choices that support a variety of reading levels and student interests. Both are natural forms of differentiation.

Differentiation Versus Tracking

Differentiation is about flexible groupings. This is the difference between differentiation and tracking. If you always keep all the strongest readers together and the weaker readers together, you are tracking. If you are able to challenge all types of students in one classroom by having everyone engage and learn from one another, you are differentiating.

DIFFERENTIATION FOR HOMOGENEOUSLY GROUPED (LEVELED) STUDENTS

Content-area classes in the junior high and high school model are less likely to be using differentiation because they are often leveled. The issue here is that even within those levels, there will be a wide range of reading abilities. As the standards are implemented, it will become clearer that even leveled classes will benefit from a differentiated approach. The most important thing to keep in mind is that there may be many factors influencing a student's arrival in your classroom:

- Is the student unmotivated?
- Did a parent waive the student into your class?
- Is the student new to school?
- Does the student have social or emotional issues that impact learning?

The list of questions could go on and on, but ultimately the student is in your classroom and requires instruction that meets his or her needs. The biggest issue for content-area teachers is that many "good students" who perform well in ELA classes may not be adept at reading nonfiction text, so a content-area teacher can see a variety of levels of comprehension and engagement that could differ from what is observed in ELA class. This makes it essential for content-area teachers to use their expertise to deliver strategy-based reading experiences. See page 56 for an example.

DIFFERENTIATION FOR HETEROGENEOUSLY GROUPED STUDENTS

Mostly the practice in middle school, heterogeneous (or mixed ability) groups can present significant challenges for teachers. In the content areas, many classroom teachers will implement differentiation by providing more work to certain students as a way of challenging them. While we understand that a challenging assignment often does require harder (and inherently more) work, we have found that MINDful reading gives all students options and opportunities. Here are some examples of how this can work in your classroom:

- *Content:* Provide a variety of different texts for students to choose from based on their interests. Share the challenge level of the books with students. Let them choose based on their interest and desire for a challenge. The method for this is discussed in the section on student selection on pages 45–47.

- *Process:* Provide different graphic organizers with tiered questions as ways of reading the book. For example, some students might read for sequence of events, while others might have the challenge of synthesizing major events with information from other sources.

- *Product:* Have students determine the method that they would like to use to share what they have learned from their text. For example, in order to show the role of women in the Space Race, students could choose to create a public service announcement (PSA), a pamphlet, a blog, and so on.

See page 57 for an example.

55

Examples of Content/Process/Product in Unit on Civil Rights

FOCUS QUESTIONS:

» *How do individuals fight for and inspire change?*

» *How is an individual's identity and character shaped?*

SAME BASIC CONTENT

All students read the same book, with supplemental readings.

» Level 3: Read *Claudette Colvin* by Phillip Hoose.

» Level 2: Read *Claudette Colvin* with supplemental articles on Rosa Parks.

» Level 1: Read *Claudette Colvin* in conjunction with *The Girl Who Fell From the Sky* (fiction) by Heidi W. Durrow.

SAME PROCESS: *All students complete the same organizer for each chapter. Choose a different organizer for each chapter.*

DIFFERENTIATED PRODUCT:

*LEVEL 3: Using evidence from the book, write a letter to Claudette Colvin and share your thoughts on her experiences as she shaped her identity/character and inspired change. Page Limit: 1 page. **Evidence from text:** minimum of 3 with page numbers cited.*

*LEVEL 2: There is going to be a national holiday for a female civil rights heroine. Who should it be for: Claudette or Rosa? Write a letter to the U.S. president explaining which woman you believe deserves the honor. Be sure to include evidence from the book about how the woman you choose shaped her identity/character and inspired change. Page Limit: 1 page. **Evidence from text:** minimum of 4 with page numbers cited.*

*LEVEL 1: **Define** identity. How did each individual develop his or her racial or ethnic identity? How do you define yours? Write a one- or two-page essay explaining your thinking. Page Limit: 2 pages. **Evidence from text:** minimum of 3 from each book with page numbers cited.*

Level 1

Dear Claudette Colvin,

After reading that book about you I realized who you were and how you made an amazing change in America. I read about your experience on the bus and discovered you were the first african american woman who attempted to make a change. In the first or second chapter I read about your arrival at Booker T Washington High School and thought it was interesting that students in the school would try to be/act like white students. "Claudette soon found that having light skin and straight hair was key to popularity at Booker T Washington. Many girls woke up early and spent hours applying hot combs to their hair, trying to straighten it to look, as some said, "almost white""(22). I was wondering why black students would try to act white and not be proud of who they are, maybe it's because they lived in fear and grew up with grandparents, parents and friends saying whites were the superior race. "The officer ordered her to get up. Again Claudette refused"(34). "One cop grabbed one of my hands and his partner grabbed the other and they pulled me straight out of my seat"(35). When I was reading I was thinking what a brave girl you were standing up for yourself and not giving up your seat without a fight. I respected you for staying in your seat. As I read on and read how you got pregnant and saw that everyone stopped looking up to you, I understood why and that's because you made a bad decision. "But what I did know is they all turned their backs on me, especially after I got pregnant. It really, really hurt"(67). After I read that I was thinking how can you feel bad after that decision you made, in my mind you brought it on yourself. So when Rosa Parks didn't get up from her seat either just like you did, she got more attention. I think she got more attention because she was older and is more mature than you are. Especially how you got pregnant everyone looking up to you, thinking of you as a leader, they all had a reason to stop paying attention to you. Citizens were looking for a responsible leader and getting pregnant wasn't something responsable so they then looked up to Rosa Parks. But, in my opinion if it weren't for you, I don't think anyone would've made a change anytime soon. You were the one who inspired people to make a change and were very brave about it. I hope you understand that people still remember you and still thank you for what you've done.

Sincerely,

Jack Ehli

Examples of Content/Process/Product in a Unit on Lincoln

FOCUS QUESTIONS:

- » *What does it mean to be free?*
- » *What are the qualities of a great leader?*

DIFFERENTIATED CONTENT

BOOK CHOICES:

- » Level 3: *Abraham Lincoln (10 Days)* by David Colbert
- » Level 2: *Chasing Lincoln's Killer* by James L. Swanson and
     Lincoln: A Photobiography by Russell Freedman
- » Level 1: *Killing Lincoln* by Bill O'Reilly
     Manhunt by James L. Swanson

SAME PROCESS: *Everyone reads his or her book and completes the same graphic organizers throughout the reading experience: Sequence of Events, Why Do You Think That?, What's Happening?, and Words From the Wise.*

SAME PRODUCT: *All students participate in a dialogue using the information they learned in their books to analyze the focus questions. They also take an assessment that has the same questions, but each student receives a page from his or her book to focus on. (A sample posttest assessment is on pages 86–87.)*

• • • • •

When you use a variety of tools and strategies to meet the needs of your students, the classroom environment becomes accessible and engaging for everyone. A MIND reading experience offers students the opportunity to read and discuss at their level and observe other students using strategies to improve their comprehension and thinking as well.

CHAPTER 4

Choosing Reading Strategy Lessons to Complement the MINDful Reading Experience

I have a passion for teaching kids to become readers, to become comfortable with a book, not daunted. Books shouldn't be daunting, they should be funny, exciting and wonderful; and learning to be a reader gives a terrific advantage.

— Roald Dahl

No matter how engaging the book, most students will not continue reading a difficult text if they do not have strategies to aid them in their comprehension. Because every student approaches a text differently, teachers need a number of methods to effectively teach reading comprehension. With MINDful reading, choosing the right text is vital, as well as identifying what students are going to focus on in both the content and reading activities. This chapter explores multiple methods for working with students before and during the reading process.

Prereading Strategies: Establishing Background Knowledge

Before students embark on a reading experience, it is important to build sufficient background knowledge. This serves two purposes: It gives students important information to aid in their comprehension of the text, and it creates a common well of information students can refer to when they discuss the text with their groups.

There are many different ways to convey essential background information. The key idea to consider is this: *What is the most important content your students need to know in order to comprehend the text?* You don't want to spend days teaching students the facts, or they will have content fatigue before they even begin the book but you also want to make sure they have enough information to make connections from the text to the background knowledge you have taught them. The introduction of content should be seen as a "teaser" to get students interested in the book and address the content expectations within your curriculum. This will aid in strengthening their overall engagement with the text.

For example, when teaching *Hiroshima* as part of a World War II unit, we determined that students needed to know about the bombing of Pearl Harbor, Japanese-American internment, Japanese war strategies, American firebombing in Japan, and dropping the atomic bomb on Hiroshima, so we created a *Hiroshima* Introduction PowerPoint presentation. Within these topics, we delivered the basic facts, including some statistics. We also made sure to include maps of Japan and the Pacific as well as before-and-after photographs of Hiroshima. (Many of these photographs showed locations cited in the text.) These images and facts helped students understand some of the ideas behind the decision to drop the bomb and gave them a visual reference of what the city looked like after the attack.

The Importance of Visualization

Visualization is an important skill for deepening comprehension, but many students have a difficult time visualizing what they read. To help students visualize:

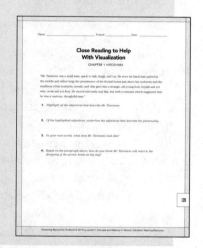

» Provide images of a real event from the nonfiction text to help students keep an image in their head as they read.

» Do a close reading of a section of the text. Look at the words the author uses and discuss what students picture in their heads based on the word choice. (See Close Reading to Help With Visualization on page 139.)

DIRECT INSTRUCTION

To establish background information using direct instruction, present information that students are required to take notes on. This is a good technique to use if you have very specific facts that you want students to know before they start reading. A PowerPoint

59

presentation is often the best way to deliver such short pieces of information. Here are a few simple rules for writing content-based notes:

- Keep notes focused
- Adhere to the 6 x 6 rule: no more than 6 bulleted items per slide and no more than 6 words per bullet
- Use visuals: photographs, short video clips, and maps

Provide students with a guided list of questions or a skeleton outline so they will be able to focus on the main points from the lesson while still learning to become independent notetakers. We have found that adolescents (especially middle school students) need a focus for their note taking; otherwise they often miss important pieces of information or write down everything in an attempt to not miss any content. Many students need the act of writing down information in order to have it stick, so it is important to not hand them the notes. Rather, students need to write the notes in their own words, such that they are applicable to future assignments and discussions. (See *Hiroshima* Introduction: Student Notes on page 140.)

CLOSE READING

Another method of introducing a unit is to start with a close reading of small chunks of text on a topic. For example, you might choose to:

- Do textbook activities for an overview of the topic
- Read a picture book aloud
- Read an article
- Review a primary document

Since these texts tend to be shorter, this is a good way to address close reading strategies as suggested in the Common Core. These strategies should focus on the Craft and Structure standards, which ask students to look at the specific vocabulary terms and the author's choice of words. These standards also expect students to examine the structure of the text as well as the variety of perspectives represented. Yet students are not just being held accountable for identifying these parts of a text; they also have to think about why an author would make these decisions and the implications these decisions have on a reader's understanding of the text.

In "Closing in on Close Reading," Nancy Boyle gives many great examples for how to approach reading these kinds of texts. She advocates for looking at the imagery, word choice, tone, and voice, and the variation in sentence length and structure. These are all components that the ELA standards also address, so this can be a great time to meet with an ELA teacher and collaborate on specific strategies to use across the curriculum. By using short documents to provide background knowledge, you can set up your students for success in their MINDful reading experience and also teach specific close reading strategies. (See Close Reading of the First Paragraph of *Hiroshima* on page 141.)

60

ANTICIPATION GUIDES

In order to facilitate metacognition (thinking about thinking), begin with a reading experience that helps students explore their initial thoughts and knowledge about an idea. By the end of a unit, they should be able to look back on this first experience and reflect on their learning and thinking as a result of the process.

An anticipation guide is a way to get students thinking about the major themes or concepts in a text, rather than just the facts. It asks students to state their position—Agree/Disagree—on a list of statements. After reading each statement, they circle the term that applies to their thinking. Make sure to stress to students that there are no "right" answers in this activity.

You can also use an anticipation guide as an informal preassessment for a unit. For example, if you notice that a group of students seems to understand the main concepts in the book already, you may choose to differentiate their instruction by asking them to look at more theme-based or global ideas in the text. On the other hand, if a group seems to struggle with the ideas on the anticipation guide, you may want to do some more direct teaching of the text with this group.

You can use this type of prereading strategy to help students begin to think about the ideas and questions they will explore throughout the unit. An anticipation guide encourages students to think beyond the facts and lets them know that they are going to be making inferences and connections and forming new ideas while they are reading.

Finally, anticipation guides can be completed individually or in groups. For example, early in the school year when students are less willing to take risks, you may choose to allow them to respond individually. We have found that by the end of the year, anticipation guides can be completed in groups in a meaningful way. You can also decide if you want students to share their thoughts with partners, their group, the whole class, or not at all.

HOW TO CREATE AN ANTICIPATION GUIDE:

- Think about your focus questions. Which ideas in the book relate to these questions? Form statements around these questions. For example, for the focus question, "How do people respond to tragedy?", you could include a statement such as the following on the guide:

  In the face of tragedy, people often prefer to work alone in order to rebuild their lives. AGREE or DISAGREE

- Decide on five to ten statements. Some of the statements can be similar so that students are challenged to really think about their own beliefs. Another question on the anticipation guide could be:

  In the face of tragedy, the individuals who overcome their struggles the quickest are the ones who work together. AGREE or DISAGREE

Teacher Tip

Google Forms and SurveyMonkey are good tools to use for creating anticipation guides. Assign an online survey for homework, and then compile student responses in a spreadsheet to review.

61

- Having statements with subtle differences pushes students to think about the two statements together. Do they believe strongly in the capacity of an individual to overcome? Or do they feel that groups of people in a community can overcome tragedy in a more timely way? Or do they believe there is not one, single way to deal with tragedy, in which case they may disagree with both statements.

- Completing the guide should be a quick activity, 10 minutes or less. Make sure the statements on it are clear and specific.

A sample anticipation guide for *Hiroshima* is shown below.

Hiroshima *Anticipation Guide*

Please circle either AGREE or DISAGREE for each of the following statements:

1. *In times of tragedy, people only look out for themselves.*

    AGREE   DISAGREE

2. *The Nazis were the only ones who killed many innocent civilians in World War II.*

    AGREE   DISAGREE

3. *In order to make people listen, you must do something drastic.*

    AGREE   DISAGREE

4. *People do not have the ability to rebuild their lives after a great disaster.*

    AGREE   DISAGREE

5. *Strangers are willing to risk their lives to help their fellow citizens.*

    AGREE   DISAGREE

6. *We can learn a lot about an event from multiple perspectives.*

    AGREE   DISAGREE

7. *Everyone involved in an event sees it the same way.*

    AGREE   DISAGREE

Extension Activity: If you want to visually see how students feel about these statements, you can create an invisible scale. For example, you might tell students that one wall in the classroom represents a "5, strongly agree" and the wall across from it is a "1, strongly disagree." The middle ground between the two represents 2, 3, and 4. Students place themselves in the room based on their response to each statement. Additionally, they must share with the class their rationale for positioning themselves as they did. You can randomly call on students to share their thinking for each statement. It gets students up and moving around, which is always a good way to break up the time spent sitting throughout the day.

Stretching Beyond the Textbook © 2014 by Lauren K. Francese and Rebecca H. Marsick, Scholastic Teaching Resources

SEE-THINK-WONDER

A strategy from one of our favorite resources, *Making Thinking Visible* by Ritchhart, Church, and Morrison, builds off the traditional K-W-L chart: What I Know—What I Want to Know—What I Learned. The first step is to ask students what perspectives and ideas they "see" within a particular topic and then extend this to what they think about it. Asking students what they *see* versus what they *know* is less definitive and gives them more freedom to take a risk with their ideas. They are not telling their classmates that they know something for sure, but rather that they see something they want to think further about. More students will engage in the conversation, allowing more ideas to be shared and discussed during the unit. Students can build off what they think to include what they want to know or wonder about. Finally, asking students to come up with new questions, instead of just stating what they've learned, enables them to synthesize and evaluate the new information and anticipate what might come next, thereby extending their thinking.

Example of See-Think-Wonder

» **See:** I see that there is a lot of destruction after the atomic bomb was dropped.

» **Think:** I think this means that many people must have been killed since there was so much devastation.

» **Wonder:** I know that some people did survive; therefore, I wonder why some people survived while others perished.

Using this process in conjunction with objects is a good way to start a conversation with students, especially reluctant readers, to get them engaged in thinking about the upcoming unit. You might start an activity by showing students an artifact or a photograph that relates to the content and ask what they see or notice about it. This discussion invites students to draw upon their background knowledge as well as personal experiences.

You can decide if you want to create a whole-class chart or have students work in groups or individually to create one. Whatever you choose, individuals or groups should share their ideas at the end of the activity. It's also important that you and/or your students keep a copy of the original chart. Students can add to the chart as they move through the text or just revisit it at the end of the book. This strategy enables students to demonstrate the evolution of their thinking, rather than just representing their thinking at the beginning of the text.

Reading Activities to Use During MIND Units

We use a variety of activities for MIND units as we make determinations about the needs of the students in our classroom. Think of these activities as your toolbox for teaching reading comprehension. Each one can be employed with any text and any type of reader. The key is to think about your focus for the text in conjunction with what you notice about your students' needs throughout the year. Here are some of our favorites:

20 Questions

This activity comes from Kelly Gallagher's book *Deeper Reading* and is best used during the first chapter of a text that is new for students. Often, the first chapter is the most difficult part of a text for students. This is where they are introduced to the author's voice and style, the setting, and characters. Nonfiction often contains difficult names, new places, and/or time periods, in addition to content-specific vocabulary.

One way to combat students' confusion is to read the first chapter with them. As you read, tell students they need to write down at least 20 questions about the text. These questions can be as simple as "Who is ___?" and "What does ___ mean?" Also encourage students to make inferences and predictions and look for evidence that supports the focus questions. By creating these questions, students will begin narrowing in on specific aspects of the text, rather than being overwhelmed by all the new information. After finishing the first chapter, have students work with their group to help one another answer as many of the questions as they can. You can then have a whole-class discussion to answer as many questions as possible. As students continue to read on their own, they should look for the answers to the remaining questions and add more questions as they arise.

The Parking Lot

Build on 20 Questions by creating a "parking lot," a space in your room where students can post anonymous questions as they read and discuss the book. At the end of our unit on World War II, students had posted several ethical questions as well as scientific questions about the impact of the bombing. Once a question was posted, students were allowed to research the answer for enrichment. For example, several students asked questions about the "black rain" that was falling throughout *Hiroshima*. With the help of the science teacher, several students researched the phenomenon and discovered that it was rain containing radioactive soot and dust. By sharing their information with the class, students demonstrated that reading can be a collaborative process.

Close Reading

Just as a short chunk of text can be used with a close reading strategy at the beginning of a unit, a book can be broken into smaller chunks and used to illuminate ideas in the text. This works especially well if you want to focus on a specific point. When we taught *Hiroshima* in the World War II unit, we asked students to differentiate among the elements of craft and structure (see chart on the next page) in their reading. We found specific parts of the text that incorporated each of these elements, and we asked students to look for examples of one or two of them at a time as they read. Once students become familiar with an element, they will begin to see it more readily in the text, and you can ask them to find more elements as they move forward (see "Close Reading of the First Paragraph of *Hiroshima*" on page 141).

Elements of Craft and Structure

FACTS	Important information located directly in the text
VOCABULARY	Unfamiliar words, as well as *how* they are used
TEXT STRUCTURE	The format the author uses to tell the story
SETTING	Time and place, as well as their importance to the story
PERSPECTIVE	Who is telling the story (1st person, 3rd person, omniscient) and the importance of perspective
INFERENCE	Applying what you know about a situation to make an informed guess
IRONY	A contrast between what is said and what is meant, an unexpected twist of fate
SYMBOLISM	When an object stands for something bigger than itself (usually an idea or something abstract)

Reading Strategies to Support Reading More Complex Texts

As texts become more complex, the reading strategies you incorporate in the MIND units must change. Many students struggle with these texts, and this is often what causes them to give up on reading. If we make it a priority to give students the strategies to read a nonfiction text, then we can help them more easily access the content and also create lifelong readers. We want to enable students to think critically, process information, and form their own ideas about a topic while reading. In *Pathways to the Common Core*, Lucy Calkins and her colleagues note that most students are "reading to accumulate information. . . . The Common Core standards ask that we shift away from this type of reading and toward helping students learn to read to develop concepts, discover ideas, and to follow (and analyze) arguments" (p. 98). The following strategies aim to do just this.

CODING AND ANNOTATING TEXT

The explicit modeling and practicing of coding and annotating text can be done throughout a unit. The types of annotations you ask students to make should be linked to the CCSS. For example, ELA-Literacy RH.6–8.1 states that in social studies and history, students should "[c]ite specific textual evidence to support analysis of primary and secondary sources." Annotations require students to be metacognitive, to think about *why* the quote they are citing is important, how it relates to the focus question, and how it helps further their understanding of the text.

65

Ultimately, you need to find engaging texts that help develop the skills outlined in the CCSS. Once you determine the skills that you want your students to use in reading the text, you can develop annotation codes with the class. It does not matter what symbols you use to code the text; the important part is that students are monitoring their thinking as they read, and the annotations help them do this. Here are examples of annotation codes:

Annotation Codes

I	I found important information that connects to and/or helps me understand the focus question.
+	I found some new information.
=	I can make a connection to the focus questions, other texts, or class discussion.
?	I'm questioning or wondering about something I just read.
C	I am reading about something I don't understand/am confused about.
P	I am reading about a perspective, and this might also be evidence of bias.

A sample coding annotation chart for *Hiroshima* appears on the next page.

Hiroshima *(World War II Unit)*

Directions: As you read, annotate the text using the codes below. Be sure to bring your book with you to class every day!

Focus Question: How do people respond to tragedy?

ANNOTATION CODE	DESCRIPTION	EXAMPLE FROM TEXT
R (REACT AND RECOVER)	This helps me answer the question: *How do people react and recover from tragedy?*	R: "One feeling they did seem to share, however, was an elated kind of community spirit." (87)
I (IMPACT)	This helps me answer the question: *How did this impact the people of Japan and America?*	I: "The Americans are dropping gasoline. They're going to set fire to us!" The weather begins to change as a result of the bombing. (38)
? (QUESTION)	I have a question that I need to ask my group.	?: Why does Father Kleinsorge wear a military uniform? (12)
* (INTERESTING OR IMPORTANT)	This is interesting or important.	*: The three stages of radiation sickness. (76)
V (VOCABULARY)	I didn't understand this phrase and needed to look it up.	V: Wasserman test (2)

MAKING INFERENCES FROM TEXT DETAILS: DIFFERENTIATED PRACTICE

Students often struggle with understanding how they can piece together textual evidence in order to make a strong inference. Requiring students to find text to support their inferences forces them to slow down their reading and think more deeply about how the facts an author presents allow them to come to a new understanding about the text. With the new demands for reading complex texts, students are going to need to read more deeply and think about their reading.

A sample plan for an evidence and inference lesson appears on pages 142–143, along with its corresponding reproducible, Evidence and Inference Class Activity sheet. In the lesson, students are asked to watch a video and record their observations, which they use to help them define *evidence* and *inference*. Then students apply the evidence and inference strategy to the text they are reading.

Teacher Tip

Pixar short videos work well with this lesson. Access them at pixar. com/short_films/home.

Stretching Beyond the Textbook © 2014 by Lauren K. Francese and Rebecca H. Marsick, Scholastic Teaching Resources

Here are differentiated samples of the Evidence and Inference Class Activity sheet for *Hiroshima*. In Level 1, we provide quotes in which the inferences are fairly obvious to our weakest readers, students read the evidence provided and write their inference based on this part of the text. In Level 2, the chosen passages are subtler in terms of determining possible inferences. Finally, the strongest readers in Level 3 are asked to be more independent and use one of their own passages as well as a longer selection of text. All of the students are practicing the same skill, using evidence to support an inference, but they are being appropriately challenged through the text they are reading. Student samples appear on page 70.

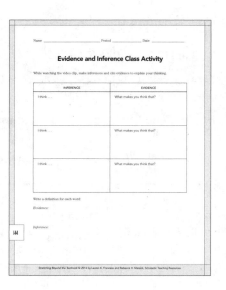

Evidence and Inference: Level I (low)

Evidence "Altogether, Miss Sasaki was left two days and two nights under the piece of propped-up roofing with her crushed leg and her two unpleasant comrades. Her only diversion was when men came to the factory air-raid shelter, and hauled corpses up out of them with ropes." (page 54)	**An inference I can make from this:**
Inference Miss Sasaki's reaction to the bombing was affected by her own physical pain, but she was also unable to comprehend this because of the great shock that overcame her.	**Evidence that will support this thinking:** * *Use pages 54 and 55.*

68

Evidence and Inference: Level 2 (middle)

Evidence	An inference I can make from this:
"Father Kleinsorge began to be thirsty in the dreadful heat, and he did not feel strong enough to go for water again. A little before noon, he saw a Japanese woman handing something out. Soon she came to him and said in a kindly voice, 'These are tea leaves, Chew them, young man, and you won't feel thirsty.' The woman's gentleness made Father Kleinsorge suddenly want to cry. For weeks, he had been feeling oppressed by the hatred of foreigners . . . this stranger's gesture made him a little hysterical." (page 52)	
Inference Read the last paragraph of Chapter 4 (page 90) and make an inference.	**Evidence that will support this thinking:**

Evidence and Inference: Level 3 (high)

Evidence	An inference I can make from this:
Evidence Choose a passage you have annotated in the text. Write it below.	
Inference Review pages 150–152. Make an inference based on the end of the book.	**Evidence that will support this thinking:**

Stretching Beyond the Textbook © 2014 by Lauren K. Francese and Rebecca H. Marsick, Scholastic Teaching Resources

Evidence and Inference
Application
Academic

Evidence	An inference I can make from this:
"Altogether, Miss Sasaki was left two days and two nights under the piece of propped up roofing with her crushed leg and her two unpleasant comrades. Her only diversion was when men came to the factory air-raid shelter, and hauled corpses up out of them with ropes." (page 54)	• she kept seeing The men pull out other bodies while no body would help her. • patient + caring I because she understands that other People need help too.
Inference Miss Sasaki's reaction to the bombing was effected by her own physical pain, but she was also unable to comprehend the even because of the great shock that overcame her.	**Some evidence that will support this thinking:** *Use page 54 and 55 "for about an hour, the truck moved over a bumpy road, and mrs Sasaki, who had become convinced that she was dulled to pain, discovered that she was not. (....) The moment one of them touched her wound. she fainted (54-55) ✓

Application
Evidence and Inference
Challenger

Evidence	An inference I can make from this:
Choose a passage you have annotated in the text. Write the quote here.... page 121-122 "These thoughts led her to an opinion that was unconventional for a hibakusha : that too much attention was paid to the power of the A-bomb, and not enough to the evil of war, not enough thought was given to the fact that warfare had indiscriminately made victims of Japanese	Miss. Sasaki, unlike other hibakusha, was thinking more about the big picture of war and moved past the tragedy of the bomb, onto blaming the Japanese for engaging government in total war. She isn't mad at America for dropping the bomb.
Inference Review page 150-152. Make an inference based on the end of the book. Based on the end of the book, I can inference that survivors of the bombing had finally closed up their wounds from the tragedy and were forgetting the horrors.	**Some evidence that will support this thinking:** 'He was slowing down a bit. His memory, like the world's was getting spotty" P 152

Application
Evidence and Inference
Scholar

Evidence	An inference I can make from this:
"Father Kleinsorge began to be thirsty in the dreadful heat, and he did not feel strong enough to go for water again. A little before noon, he saw a Japanese woman handing something out. Soon she came to him and said in a kindly voice, 'These are tea leaves. Chew them, young man, and you won't feel thirsty.' The woman's gentleness made Father Kleinsorge suddenly want to cry. For weeks, he had been feeling oppressed by the hatred of foreigners...this stranger's gesture made him a little hysterical." (page 52)	Before the bomb people weren't accepting to one another if they were different but after the bomb every one came to help one another. I
Inference Read the last paragraph of chapter 4 (page 90) and make an inference... The Children were able to take the horrors of that day that changed his life o life lesson because they were children they had totally different perspectives than an adult would have	**Some evidence that will support this thinking:** "on the surface, their recollections, months after the disaster were an exhilarating adv." (90) showing that it was like an adventure and life lesson but the kids didn't realize the seriousness of the horrible disaster

READING WITH A PURPOSE

Students benefit from direct instruction in reading with a purpose. This strategy helps them find success in understanding focus questions. Many students get bogged down reading every word and forget that they are supposed to be thinking about using the focus questions to read thematically.

The Common Core State Standards ask students to read with a specific idea in mind, looking for the author's purpose as well as the central idea in a text:

- *RI.8.2:* Determine an author's point of view or purpose in a text and analyze how the author acknowledges and responds to conflicting evidence or viewpoints.

- *RI.8.6:* Determine a central idea of a text and analyze its development over the course of the text, including its relationship to supporting ideas; provide an objective summary of the text.

Good focus questions for a topic will naturally connect to the author's purpose as well as the central idea of the text. The focus questions will also allow students to think beyond the text itself, helping them to make stronger inferences, connections, and predictions.

Purposeful Reading

This activity helps students think about how they read and then shift their thinking to a more focused process. The follow-up activity gets students thinking about how to read with purpose in the real world.

For the text you choose, create a Reading With Purpose reproducible like the sample shown on the next page.

- Break an article into two or more sections.

- At the end of each section of text, write a purpose question for the section and ask students to use text evidence to support their answers.

- Close with a series of questions that ask students to reflect on their reading.

To introduce this activity, write the word *purpose* on the board. Then start with a quick discussion of the word. In the example below, we asked students to read an article titled "John Lewis Continues the Fight."

Teacher: *After reading the definition of* purpose, *think about your own interpretation of this word. What does purpose mean to you? In your life, when do you do something with purpose?* (Ask a few students to respond. Then distribute the text and give a Reading With Purpose reproducible to each student.)

Something that strong readers do is read with a purpose. Often, the amount of information in a text can become so overwhelming that we want to give up because we just don't "get" it all. This is a common reaction to more complex nonfiction, like the text we're

(continued on page 74)

71

Stretching Beyond the Textbook © 2014 by Lauren K. Francese and Rebecca H. Marsick, Scholastic Teaching Resources

Reading With a Purpose

PURPOSE (*noun*): *something set up as an object or end to be attained, an intention*

Define *purpose* in your own words: _____

_____

Read the text below.

John Lewis Continues the Fight

John Lewis's great-great-grandfather registered to vote when he was freed from slavery after the Civil War—and he voted, too. Then Jim Crow laws were passed in 1876 that segregated the South and kept African Americans from enjoying their constitutional rights. Until President Lyndon Johnson signed the Voting Rights Act on August 6, 1965, neither John Lewis nor his parents enjoyed the same voting rights as their ancestor did.

Several events influenced the passage of the Voting Rights Act, and John Lewis was present at each one. In 1961, he joined the Freedom Riders. Thousands of Freedom Riders, black and white, rode buses into the segregated South, breaking the Jim Crow laws. During these rides, Lewis received the first of many beatings.

In 1963, Lewis helped plan the March on Washington. Hundreds of thousands heard his fiery speech: "We want our freedom, and we want it now!" Two years later, on a quiet Sunday, Lewis led a march from Selma to Montgomery, Alabama, to protest the disenfranchisement of African Americans.

Alabama state troopers met the 600 marchers at the Edmund Pettus Bridge. As they watched the events on TV, millions of Americans were horrified to see the marchers being beaten by troopers wielding bullwhips, batons, and hoses wrapped in barbed wire. Almost a hundred marchers were injured—including John Lewis, whose skull was fractured. This day of shame became known as "Bloody Sunday."

Purpose: Why did John Lewis fight for voters' rights, and how did he do so?

Highlight parts of the text that relate to this purpose.

Which evidence that you highlighted tells the reader about John Lewis's fight for voters' rights?

Write the evidence below. _____

_____

_____

_____

72

Read the text below.

Today, John Lewis sits in the congress as a U.S. Representative from Georgia, but he remains vigilant about protecting voters' rights. Many states have enacted strict voter ID laws since 2010. From the House floor, Lewis has warned, "We must not step backward to another dark period in our history. The vote is the most powerful nonviolent tool we have in a democratic society."

Purpose: *Why does John Lewis continue to fight for voters' rights?*

Highlight parts of the text that relate to this purpose.

Which evidence that you highlighted tells the reader why John Lewis continues to fight for voters' rights?

Write the evidence below. _____

_____

_____

● ● ● ● ●

How did reading with purpose guide your reading? _____

_____

_____

What did you learn about the perspectives in the article? _____

_____

_____

Why do you think reading text with a purpose will be helpful to you?_____

_____

_____

73

Stretching Beyond the Textbook © 2014 by Lauren K. Francese and Rebecca H. Marsick, Scholastic Teaching Resources

reading today. However, I'm going to give you a free pass to not "get" everything. Today, we are going to practice reading with a purpose. You're going to read the article thinking only about the question posed on the reproducible. If something else in the article strikes you as interesting, please mark it, but you are only responsible for being able to answer the questions on the handout when you have finished the article.

FOLLOW-UP ACTIVITY: READING WITH PURPOSE IN THE REAL WORLD

Students should understand that many adults choose to read texts that relate to their professional lives or are driven by personal interests. The way that we gain information, whether it is online or from books, magazines, and so on, is to purposefully look for something to read. There are many ways to introduce this activity to students, including going through it question by question. However, if you feel your class can do this more independently, you can introduce it as shown below.

Teacher: *How many of you know someone who is a professional—someone who has a job in which he or she is required to know certain information in order to perform the task at hand? I want you to think about the kind of reading that this person might do. Does anyone have an example?* (Discuss students' responses.)

In the following activity, you're going to think about a profession that interests you. I want you to really ponder the type of reading that this someone in the profession might have to do to be successful. This is an example of how adults have to read with a purpose in their lives.

Reading With Purpose in the Real World
Choose a profession that interests you.

Profession: _____

What does this person need to know about in order to do his or her job well?

_____

_____

Identify an example of a nonfiction text that person might need to read for his or her job. _____

_____

Find an example of nonfiction text that a person in the profession might have to read. Bring the example to class.

74

Purpose:

Explain the purpose a person in this profession would have for reading this example text.

Purpose: _____

_____

Group Share:

Share your text and purpose with your group.

On your own, write a short response: How do people read with purpose in the real world? Give other examples. _____

_____

CREATE YOUR OWN PURPOSEFUL READING ASSIGNMENTS

In the early stages of practicing this reading strategy, make sure to pick a text in which the answers to the posed questions are very evident in the text. Remember, the questions should not be about finding facts, but rather should focus on an idea or theme that the class has been discussing. The easiest way to have students read with a purpose is to use the focus questions established at the beginning of the unit. It is helpful to have a question for reflection at the end of a short text to remind students that they are reading with a purpose. It can be as simple as the following question: *Reflect: How did reading with a purpose guide your understanding of the text today?* Here are more options for creating activities related to reading with purpose.

. . . .

About Purpose

PURPOSE (noun): something set up as an object or end to be attained, an intention

Describe an activity you are involved in that has a clear purpose.

What is the activity?

What is the purpose? How do you know this?

. . . .

About Purpose

PURPOSE (noun): something set up as an object or end to be attained, an intention

Describe an activity you are involved in that has a clear purpose. Describe an activity that you are involved in that has no clear purpose. Think about a time when you have said to yourself, "What's the point of this?"

What is the activity? Why do you think it has no clear purpose?

What are your feelings or attitudes toward this activity?

. . . .

About Purpose

PURPOSE *(noun): something set up as an object or end to be attained, an intention*

Describe an activity you are involved in that has a clear purpose. Being purposeful (or having a purpose) is central to success academically and in life. But is it more than just attaining something or having an intention? Write your thoughts below.

Using your own thoughts and reflections, write your own definition of purpose below.

Reading With a Purpose

READING WITH A PURPOSE: *a goal, intention, and focus that a reader establishes when beginning a book or text*

The purpose for reading is best shaped as a question, but it can also be a clear statement that defines the reader's goals moving forward.

HERE IS THE REAL SECRET: *When you practice reading with purpose, you are more efficient, more engaged, and can prioritize important information. But even better, when you develop routines for reading with purpose, you will begin to develop as a deep reader and thinker.*

Read this article with purpose and think about this question: How does deep reading benefit you and society as a whole?

(Choose a nonfiction article to insert.)

Identifying Key Details: Shopping in a Text

Another essential reading strategy is being able to identify important information while reading. In the following activity, students are given a shopping list of important things—details, evidence, and information—to find in their reading. This activity should be introduced after doing a few lessons on evidence and inference. Before asking students to work on their own, have them brainstorm some of the strategies they used to find evidence in the text to support their inferences.

Teacher: *Have you ever walked into a grocery store looking for a specific item or into a clothing store for a specific piece of apparel? If you have, you know that there is a strategy for finding what you want or need. You have to be persistent, look at labels, sizes, numbers, colors, and other details. When you discover that you can't find an item, you have to ask for help! This is precisely the way good readers approach a book, article, or any other type of text.*

You can use this activity with a first chapter or as a formative assessment in the middle of a unit if you feel that students are not reading closely enough or struggling with the text. Here's how to set it up:

76

Stretching Beyond the Textbook © 2014 by Lauren K. Francese and Rebecca H. Marsick, Scholastic Teaching Resources

■ Choose the text you want students to work with. Try not to pick something that is too short—it could be a chapter or a section of a chapter, but it needs to be challenging enough to require them to persist in their reading.

■ Create a shopping list of items for students to highlight as they read the text. You're not asking student to find facts. Rather, they have to find information and apply it to the ideas you are asking them to think about. Providing page numbers can help them focus on certain sections of the text, and it makes the activity less stressful, especially for struggling readers. However, if you think your students are ready to tackle this activity without that guidance, go for it.

Below are two examples of shopping lists. The first one is a generic list that can be applied to most texts. The second one is specific to *Claudette Colvin: Twice Toward Justice* by Philip Hoose.

Shopping List

DIRECTIONS: As you read Chapter 1, highlight the evidence (words, phrases, pictures, captions) for each item on your list. Cross off an item once you have found it in the text. If you can't find an item, ask for help!

1. People introduced in the first chapter
2. Important information the author provides to introduce you to the topic
3. Key terms presented to the reader and their definitions (how the author explains them)
4. What evidence did you find here that helps you understand the focus question?

Shopping List

DIRECTIONS: As you read Chapter 1, highlight the evidence (words, phrases, pictures, captions) for each item on your shopping list. Cross off an item once you have found it in the text. If you can't find an item, ask for help!

1. Claudette Colvin's new learning (page 3)
2. Role of Jim Crow laws in the South (pages 3–4)
3. Who was Jim Crow? (pages 4–5)
4. The experience of riding buses for black passengers (pages 7–9)
5. What "change was in the wind" means (page 9)

Stretching Beyond the Textbook © 2014 by Lauren K. Francese and Rebecca H. Marsick, Scholastic Teaching Resources

Highlighting forces students to focus on the text. Try to have many different colors of highlighters for students to choose from and let them color-code the text if they want to. You can create an answer key for this activity so students can compare what they highlighted for each item. They can reflect on whether they highlighted too little or too much and see their errors. Have students shop around to explore what they are reading, monitor their progress, and support them when they need it. By initiating this practice early in a unit, you can gather information to tailor instruction to small groups and individual students. For example, if students struggle with explaining what "change in the wind" means, you know you need to teach how to use context clues in the text to help them understand expressions.

Author's Purpose/Point of View

When students read, they need to make inferences about the author's underlying message. This is true for both fiction and nonfiction. When reading fiction, many of the inferences students make will be about the main character. But there are also "characters" in narrative nonfiction. A reader needs to understand that the actions, thoughts, and dialogue that an author uses to identify characters in nonfiction also help convey facts and tell a story. The following activity asks students to look at many of the same underlying ideas about character development that they have studied in ELA class; this time they are viewing it through the nonfiction lens.

WHO SAID IT?

This lesson helps students understand how to read narrative nonfiction and implement appropriate strategies with narrative text in general.

Stretching Beyond the Textbook © 2014 by Lauren K. Francese and Rebecca H. Marsick, Scholastic Teaching Resources

Who Said It? How? Why? How Do You Know?

Whenever you read, you make inferences (reasonable guesses) about the author's underlying message. This is true for both fiction and nonfiction. When you read narrative nonfiction, many of the inferences you make will be about the "character" of the piece.

Directions: Read Chapter 6 from Jack Gantos's *Hole in My Life*, taking response notes in the margin.

Identify: Text structures, Appositives

What is your reaction to Jack Gantos's story? _____

_____

_____

_____

Who is Jack Gantos? *Review the annotations you made while reading the selection. Then use the chart below to help you decide what you know about the author and what you can infer.* _____

_____

_____

What I know about Jack Gantos (*evidence from the text*)	What I've inferred about Jack Gantos

• • • • •

Through the consistent implementation of these strategies, students will internalize reading strategies and begin applying them more independently. The internalization and application of these strategies fosters enhanced classroom discussion about texts and the content in general.

Stretching Beyond the Textbook © 2014 by Lauren K. Francese and Rebecca H. Marsick, Scholastic Teaching Resources

CHAPTER 5

Assessing Comprehension Through Whole-Class Dialogue

> *Words mean more than what is set down on paper. It takes the human voice to infuse them with deeper meaning.*
>
> —Maya Angelou

Meaningful dialogue takes place throughout the MINDful reading process. As students progress through a book, small-group discussions support and target the needs of a range of readers in your classroom. At the culmination of a unit, students need to participate in a final assessment to determine both their understanding of the focus questions and the text's content in relation to the curriculum. The most appropriate activity to assess this is through a whole-class dialogue in which students have the opportunity to share their thoughts about the focus questions and present connections, questions, and new ideas with the class.

The Dialogue Experience

A culminating assessment in many content-area classes involves a test or an essay. Tests and written work are valid ways to assess student learning, and using texts for an essay at the end of the unit is certainly an option, but direct involvement with dialogue is a powerful experience for students. Even if you decide to have students write a paper or take a test, use the dialogue to wrap up the experience.

The most important thing to instill in your students is that a dialogue is not a debate. The dialogue should be established as a safe space where students share their thinking about the focus questions and the content they have explored throughout the small-group discussions. During the dialogue, students are expected to make inferences and draw conclusions using evidence from the text and previous discussions. Most important, they are allowed to change their perspectives throughout the dialogue.

As students begin the dialogue, make sure they know the following:

- This is not a debate. There are no winners or losers, just good thinkers.

- Doing well in a dialogue requires a combination of speaking *and* listening skills.

- Focus questions provide a framework for the dialogue. The dialogue always begins with these questions, and students can pose new questions as they come to mind.

- The teacher is just a listener. This dialogue belongs to students.

Dialogue and the CCSS

Dialogues target the CCSS Speaking and Listening strands as students use textual evidence to collaborate throughout the MINDful reading process.

COMPREHENSION AND COLLABORATION *Speaking and Listening Strand 1*	• Engage in a range of collaborative discussions • Arrive prepared for discussions • Pose questions that connect to the ideas of others • Acknowledge new information and connect it to existing views/ideas • Identify relevant evidence and sound reasoning
PRESENTATION OF KNOWLEDGE AND IDEAS *Speaking and Listening Strand 2*	• Support claims and findings with evidence • Use sound and valid reasoning • Use appropriate eye contact, volume, and pronunciation

ASSESSMENT OF THE DIALOGUE

Assessment (grading) for the dialogue is divided into three parts:

- *Dialogue Preparation Sheet:* The teacher generates a preparation sheet that students complete and bring to the whole-class dialogue.

- *Dialogue Participation:* The teacher uses scripting and notes to evaluate a student's level of contribution to the dialogue.

- *Reflection:* The teacher provides a prompt for students that encourages them to reflect upon their MINDful reading experience.

Stretching Beyond the Textbook © 2014 by Lauren K. Francese and Rebecca H. Marsick, Scholastic Teaching Resources

Preparation for the Whole-Class Dialogue

The whole-class dialogue begins with student preparation. Before a dialogue, students complete a Dialogue Preparation Sheet in which they respond to the focus questions using evidence from the text and prepare their own questions to bring to the discussion. Students need to include textual evidence and make inferences on their Dialogue Preparation Sheets; however, they typically need some support and guidance early in the school year. The completed sheet is a part of their final grade, so have students begin work on it during class so they can ask clarifying questions about the process.

Your design of the preparation sheet can evolve with the development of your students' ideas and thinking as they read. When developing a preparation sheet, always include the focus questions and ask students to create two or three questions of their own. They should always be thinking about how they might respond to these questions since they can refer to their notes during the dialogue.

The focus questions establish a framework and a common thread for students as they enter the discussion. These are the questions that students have been exploring throughout the unit, and it is very important to bring their responses to the whole-class discussion at the end of the unit. However, you can also incorporate questions that students may have been thinking about throughout their reading without even realizing it. For example, with the World War II unit, students focused on different perspectives in response to tragedy while reading, but they started making personal connections, which they talked about in their small-group discussions. In order to bring those ideas forward, we included a question related to empathy on the Dialogue Preparation Sheet for the unit. In the Space Race unit, we asked students to focus on the impact of competition, but in their small-group discussions, many students saw connections to current events and civil rights. These elements were important to include in the organizer. See sample Dialogue Preparation Sheets on pages 145 and 146.

One student's completed Dialogue Preparation Sheet about the space race during which she learned about female astronauts appears on the next page.

82

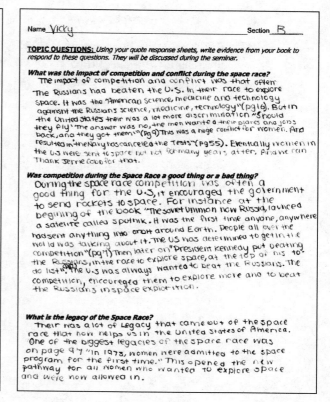

Name Vicky　　　　　　　　　　　　**Section** B

SPACE RACE
Socratic Seminar Preparation Sheet
THIS WILL BE TURNED IN AS PART OF YOUR GRADE!

Directions: Using evidence/excerpts from the text, develop questions to ask and discuss during the seminar. Remember people read **different** books so you need to think of a question that could be answered by any book that anyone read. The essential questions you have been looking at are examples of questions like this.

OPEN-ENDED QUESTIONS:
Write 3-4 insightful questions with more then one answer that can be answered by using any book. (You are basically coming up with your own essential questions)

1) • If Jerrie Cobb had put the fight up on trying to go up in to space why didn't she go instead of Collins with her pin?

2) If women can go to space in Russia then why not move their and go to space with Russia?

YOUR RESPONSES TO YOUR QUESTIONS:
Write your responses to the questions you came up with.

1) Although Jerrie Cobb never got to experience, she stated that "It was her hopes and dreams that went hurting into space with Collins, along for the ride" (pg.102) Lady Jerrie Cobb was to old to go into space but she gave a pin to Collins to take to space

2) This is because they most likely wanted to go to space with their own country so they can say that they made this happen and that the reason why they are in space is because they deserve it. They earned their spot.

Name Vicky　　　　　　　　　　　　**Section** B

TOPIC QUESTIONS: Using your quote response sheets, write evidence from your book to respond to these questions. They will be discussed during the seminar.

What was the impact of competition and conflict during the space race?
The impact of competition and conflict was that often The Russians had beaten the U.S. in their race to explore space. It was the "American science, medicine and technology against the Russians science, medicine, technology" (pg18). But in the United States their was a lot more discrimination "Should they Fly" "The answer was no, the men wanted their planes and jobs back, and they got them" (pg9) This was a huge conflict for women. And resulted in the Navy ro cancelled the Tests" (pg55). Eventually women in the US were sent to space but not for many years after. And we can Thank Jerrie Cobb for that.

Was competition during the Space Race a good thing or a bad thing?
During the space race competition was often a good thing for the U.S, it encouraged the government to send rockets to space. For instance at the beginning of the book "The soviet Union now Russia, launced a satelite called spotnik. It was the first time anyone, anywhere had sent anything into orbit around Earth. People all over the world was talking about it. The US was determined to get in the competition" (pg7) Then later on "President Kennedy put beating the Russians, in the race to explore space, at the top of his to-do list" (pg8). The U.S was always wanted to beat the Russians. The competition, encouraged them to explore more and to beat the Russians in space exploration.

What is the legacy of the Space Race?
Their was a lot of legacy that came out of the space race that now helps us in the United States of America. One of the biggest legacies of the space race was on page 97 "In 1973, women were admitted to the space program for the first time." This opened the new pathway for all women who wanted to explore space and were now allowed in.

Student Participation in the Dialogue

On the day of the whole-class dialogue, students bring in their completed Dialogue Preparation Sheets and books. Desks (or just chairs if you have somewhere else to put desks) should be arranged in two concentric circles. Half of the class sits in an inner circle, and the other half sits in a surrounding outer circle. The role of students in the inner circle is to engage in thoughtful dialogue about the focus questions and student-generated questions. The role of students in the outer circle is to listen to the dialogue, take notes, and be prepared to give feedback to the students in the inner circle when their dialogue time is up. Here's how the dialogue process is structured:

- Students enter the room and sit in their assigned circle. The best way to do this for student-selected texts is to mix students so that multiple books will be represented in each circle. For whole-class texts, assign placement by splitting your class list alphabetically or mixing students based on reading abilities in order to have a varied representation of levels in each circle.

- Tell students in the inner circle to take out their Dialogue Preparation Sheets and books.

- Give students in the outer circle a sheet of paper. Tell them to make notes about the content and character of the discussion. Choose one or two things for the outer circle to watch for and make notes about what you feel would best support the spirit of collaboration and participation in your classroom.

83

Stretching Beyond the Textbook © 2014 by Lauren K. Francese and Rebecca H. Marsick, Scholastic Teaching Resources

- Students in the inner circle begin their discussion while students in the outer circle listen and make their notes.

- When the inner circle is finished with its dialogue (you can set time limits based on your school schedule), the outer circle gives feedback to the inner circle on the content and character of the discussion.

- The groups swap places, and students now in the inner circle initiate their discussion. Emphasize that the inner circle must not simply repeat the ideas from the first group's dialogue, but rather students should build on those ideas during their dialogue.

- When the inner circle finishes, students in the outer circle give feedback on the content and character of the discussion.

- During the dialogues, the teacher makes notes about the dialogue topics, questions, and ideas that emerge. At the end of the dialogue, wrap up by highlighting some of the most salient points and commend students on quality collaboration and participation.

The Blindfolded Dialogue: A Story From Lauren's Classroom

One year, I had a group of students who were very mixed in ability, interest, and motivation. It was a large class, and students talked over each other and were even unkind at times. I tried everything I could to get them to have a thoughtful discussion without the high-achievers posturing and the less-motivated kids being totally disengaged, but continued to struggle as the year progressed. One morning, two girls walked into my room and asked if we could have a talk. They shared with me their frustration about the class dynamics and said that they really wanted to have a good discussion. The saving grace in this talk was that they actually had faith in their classmates and thought that a good discussion was possible. I asked them if they had any suggestions for me, and one of the girls said, "I have no idea what to do. I just wish everyone in this class could be blind for the day. Then they would have to listen to each other."

This was a light bulb moment for me. I ran out that afternoon and bought blindfolds. I walked into class the next day and handed one to each student. They all put on the blindfolds. I presented a focus question to begin the whole-class dialogue, and an amazing thing emerged: deep thinking. Students took turns with limited intervention from me. By taking away their ability to see each other's reactions and judgment, I was able to see that all the students in this class had something truly meaningful to share. Adolescents can hide their thinking behind their school persona. Great discussion and thinking can emerge in a blindfolded dialogue in classes with a powerful social dynamic.

Stretching Beyond the Textbook © 2014 by Lauren K. Francese and Rebecca H. Marsick, Scholastic Teaching Resources

Observation Sheet Options

Try to focus on "content" and "character" when determining what students will look for when they are in the outer circle. Here are some ideas:

» List examples of your peers' collaborating during this dialogue.

» Note who has the most opportunities to speak and who might not have been included and brought into the dialogue.

» Write down new or interesting ideas that emerged, and the person or people responsible for arriving at the idea.

» Describe an idea or perspective that differed from yours or surprised you.

Teacher Tip

Keep in mind that you have been differentiating your instruction for students throughout the reading process. The dialogue occurs when all of the students come together and share what they have learned. Even if students read different books or some students had to read excerpts, everyone has thought about the focus questions and explored the content. With differentiation, you have leveled the playing field for the whole-class dialogue, and everyone will have something to share.

GRADING

Since the dialogue is a free-flowing exchange among the students, it can often be a challenge to effectively grade and keep track of student participation and the quality of that participation. Having a scoring chart can help resolve this. Sometimes, students choose not to speak during the seminar, or there happens to be a lot of very involved students who take up the speaking time. It is important that students who don't have much opportunity to speak are still awarded some credit for being active listeners. And they will always have the opportunity to write about what they would have liked to say in their reflection paper.

Completed Teacher Scoring Sheets

Stretching Beyond the Textbook © 2014 by Lauren K. Francese and Rebecca H. Marsick, Scholastic Teaching Resources

The Scoring Sheet shown on page 148 is also a good tool for monitoring students' progress throughout the year, and the more students participate in these types of activities, the more comfortable they will become. Using this tool makes it manageable to chart students' development in the three areas described on the rubric without having to go back through a stack of papers or rubrics. The Dialogue Grading Rubric appears on page 149. This can be easily filled in once the dialogue is over and the Dialogue Preparation Sheets are turned in.

ASSESSMENT BEYOND THE DIALOGUE

If the whole-class dialogue does not seem to produce enough concrete data or insight into students' reading skills, you may choose to design a posttest for the unit. Below is an example from the Lincoln unit. Students used their notes from class to help them answer questions about a passage from their selected text.

Lincoln Posttest Assessment

DIRECTIONS: You may use your graphic organizers to answer the questions below. You must use specific details from the selection of texts provided you AND your notes. Please write your answers on a separate sheet of lined paper. Make sure you number your responses.

When you are finished, attach your organizers to your test.

1. What does the word "emancipation" mean? How is it discussed in your text?

2. What came before this passage and what came after? How do you know? Be specific.

86

3. Highlight the part of the text that shows evidence to answer the focus question: *What does it mean to be free?* You should also pull in information from other sections of the text to support your highlighting.

4. Highlight part of the text that shows evidence to answer the focus question: *What are the qualities of a great leader?* You should also pull in information from other sections of the text to support your highlighting.

5. What is an inference you can make from this passage? What specific evidence is there to support your inference? Use a direct quote. Explain how this evidence connects to your inference.

Reflection

After the whole-class dialogue, students need to reflect on the entire MINDful reading experience. The reflection should be the same for each student regardless of what (or how) he or she read during the unit. Reflection assignments should be open and flexible and allow students to reflect on all elements of the unit. In a reflection, students do the following:

- Describe their experience with reading the text.
- Describe their experience as a participant in the whole-class dialogue.
- Explain the new learning, ideas, and/or realizations that emerged from reading and discussing the text. This includes any new questions and comments students may have about the content.

The final reflection at the culmination of the MIND unit is essential because:

- students need the time and opportunity to reflect on the focus questions.
- students revisit the text, draw meaning, and make connections.
- students can share their personal thoughts and feelings about the process, book selections, and dialogue experience.
- students can set goals for future reading experiences.

At the conclusion of the World War II unit, students were prompted to reflect by answering the following question: *In one or two words or a short statement, how would you describe your experience reading and discussing Hiroshima over the last two weeks? Explain, using specific examples from the book and your discussions.*

In the sample reflections from the World War II unit on the next page, each student demonstrates an understanding of the text, the focus question, and reflects on how the dialogue was an important part of the experience.

87

Student Sample 1

Reading Hiroshima *for the past two weeks has been an eye-opening experience. There were many aspects of the book that I was surprised about after reading it, including learning about human kindness, perseverance, and resiliency. Before reading the book, I thought I understood about how the atomic bomb affected people in Hiroshima and Nagasaki. But, I now understand the full extent of the damage America caused. But, amidst the disaster and terror after the bombing, there was still humanity. . . . Lastly, resiliency had a great influence in* Hiroshima. *All of the different characters had basic resiliency, since they had to bounce back from a tragedy like the atomic bomb attack to get back on their feet and continue with their life. Father K and Miss Sasaki stood out to me in this section. Father Kleinsorge fought radiation sickness and other serious ailments caused by the atomic bomb, all while working and helping other people and bomb survivors. He had an impact on Miss Sasaki, who was in deep depression. Father K impressed me immensely due to how he recovered. He didn't just recover from the tragedy, he helped others recover too! To me, that was amazing. Miss Sasaki also recovered with flying colors. After being abandoned and crushed by books, told she would die, and fighting depression, she came back. With Father K's help, she recovered so well that she converted to Catholicism and became a nun to help others. When I remember how she was just lying there, depressed and dying under books, to how she ended up helping others, her transformation and bounce-back ability was amazing.*

Student Sample 2

Reading Hiroshima *was not very interesting but discussing it was much better. I think that reading* Hiroshima *by John Hersey was not of my best interest because I felt that Hersey did not include enough emotion for me to read the book. Although it would have changed the book drastically, I think it would have been for the better of the book. The six perspectives of the book didn't have any outside perspective of the tragedy, I think that an outside perspective would've helped me relate to the tragedy. Although I still read the book I was resisting in certain parts, when the woman's hand fell off like a glove and Hersey showed no emotion. I thought if he had shown emotion it would've added to the empathy of the reader and therefore would've created a better book if the reader could've put themselves in the 6 perspective's shoes. . . . The one big thing that I did learn from the book is history is written by the victor. I figured this out when I realized how big of a tragedy Hiroshima was compared to Pearl Harbor and 9/11. In history we learn about Pearl Harbor and how big of a tragedy and how it killed about 2,000 people that not even close in perspective to 100,000 civilians, yet our country is taught that 9/11 and Pearl Harbor was the end all be all of tragedy's. This is not right because Hiroshima should be changed in our history and should not be learned about in the view to end a war but in the view that 9/11 is learned about that civilians were killed. . . . Although I did not enjoy reading the book like I wish I did, I really enjoyed the socratic seminar (dialogue) because I felt like it made me look at the book differently, someone said, "I think it would've ruined the book if Hersey included emotion because it would've created a bias." I thought that it was very interesting to hear that someone had the complete opposite opinion that I had and I could understand that opinion too. I also started to come to conclusions about the essential question, like in the middle of the discussion I thought that John Hersey's reaction to tragedy was writing this book and I felt I started to like the book a lot more. I would like to do a [dialogue] for many more subjects because it helps me look at ideas differently.*

Teacher Tip

Here are some ideas for reflection questions:

» Choose one word or a short statement that describes your experience. Use evidence from the text and discussion to explain your thinking.

» What is the most important new understanding you developed as a result of reading this book? Use evidence from the text and discussion to explain your thinking.

» Did reading and discussing this book make you want to learn and/or discover more about the content or a related idea?

» What have you learned about yourself after reading this book? Use evidence from the text and discussion to explain your thinking.

USING FOCUS QUESTIONS

The biggest mistake in designing a reflection paper is making it too open-ended. Broad, free-flowing reflections tend to solicit vague and generic responses—the kind of responses that kids think their teacher wants to hear. While you will still get stock answers at times, structuring reflection around the unit focus questions will promote thoughtful and evidence-based reflection. Below are some reflections from the World War II unit (whole-class and student-selected models) related to the focus questions. Students express their own individual reflections about the text but have clearly gone back to the text and used evidence to support their thinking.

Focus Question: How does your perspective shape/influence your world?

I would say that my experience reading <u>Hiroshima</u> by John Hersey was a light bulb moment for me. I never realized how terrible war was for civilians, along with the soldiers. Also, I had always heard about the bombings of Hiroshima and Nagasaki from the American side. I had learned that the United States dropped 2 atomic bombs on Japan and that had ended the war. But I learned what it was like for the Japanese, and it changed my whole view of the event. I never knew how much suffering the Japanese had to endure.

89

Focus Question: How can multiple perspectives influence the telling of history?

Seeing multiple perspectives I realized that not everyone has the same opinions on things. For example, in chapter three, Tanimoto begs Doctor Sasaki to help the most wounded. But Reverend T replies, "In an emergency like this', he said, as if he were reciting a manual, 'the first task is to help as many as possible—to save as many lives as possible. There is no hope for the heavily wounded. They will die. We can't bother with them" (Hersey, 50). This quote represents Mr. Sasaki's opinions on how to take care of this issue. But from a citizens standpoint, Tanimoto does not agree. These are his friends that are dying, they must be helped first, so they don't die. But Mr. Sasaki is saying that they will die anyways, so we must cure the ones that will live. Lastly, because of all the factors that might go on during ones lifetime, the perspectives on the bomb may be altered, therefore, people studying this time period in the future, may never know what actually happened, because everyone has a different outlook on the tragedy.

Focus Question: How do multiple perspectives influence the way nations interact?

I finished the book with more questions than answers. Sarah Kay ended her speech saying, "This isn't my first time here. This isn't my last time here. These aren't the last words I will share. But just in case, I'm trying my hardest to get it right this time." I believe that tragedies like Hiroshima, Nagasaki and 9/11 are the only way to promote world peace. They are perfect examples of what world peace can prevent. I know that the countries around the world have tried to settle their differences and become peaceful. And I know they have failed. But maybe this time, I hope they try their hardest get it right.

Focus Question: What do multiple perspectives show us about how people deal with tragedy?

Over the course of the past two weeks, I learned that people can do extraordinary things when faced with extreme tragedy. Six characters reacted and recovered to the tragedy of the dropping of the atomic bomb throughout the book in many different ways. I not only realized the true horror that the Japanese people were forced to endure, but I also realized that Hiroshima, was the first graphic exposure to an event in history that I have read about. This novel is unlike many chapters in a history textbook, because the writing was taken directly hand in hand with emotions from the events in history. I felt that Hersey was able to channel the six brave and strong-willed souls from their tellings, to the text, and then finally, to me. I empathized with all of the characters at least once throughout the book. It was a immense eye opener to the level of goriness and depression wars truly entitle.

Stretching Beyond the Textbook © 2014 by Lauren K. Francese and Rebecca H. Marsick, Scholastic Teaching Resources

REVISITING THE TEXT AND SHARING PERSONAL THOUGHTS

Reflection is powerful for students and allows them to bring together all of their thinking in one place. Since the dialogue takes place for a limited amount of time, the reflection gives students a chance to share some of the questions or ideas that emerged but that they might not have had an opportunity to share. Sometimes the dialogue may go in a certain direction, and a student feels there wasn't a good time to pose his or her question or idea. The reflection provides the forum for students to incorporate those ideas. This process is validating for students, and in an atmosphere where they feel their opinions are valued, they will demonstrate deep thinking.

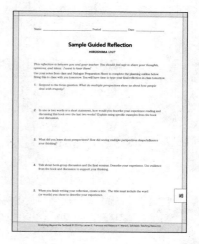

Since participation in the dialogue and completion of the reflection can be equally weighted for their grade, students have many opportunities to see success in the final assessment. Sample guided reflections appear on pages 150 and 151.

GOAL SETTING

Creating opportunities for adolescents to set goals for the future can help you better understand students' needs and build relationships with them. Students reflect about what they would change or do better the next time, and when that time comes, look at their previous reflection and talk about how it will inform book (or level) selection this time. Students often forget about their goal setting, so having it in writing is helpful! Here are some examples:

Next time to improve the book club experience I want to set pages for each day. I felt I was cramming in all of the pages the last day and dividing it up by day makes better sense. But other than that, I really do not know what I would change. I loved my book, my group participated and we really got the work done. It was a rather fun unit for social studies and I am happy I got to read the book that I did to learn about such a cool period of time.

And again, since every class has a unique dialogue experience and students have to engage in active listening and use evidence from the text, there is a lot going on. Students need to have a chance in their reflections to share what they would have said, ran out of time to share, or thought about after leaving the discussion. This creates a sense of fairness for students and lets them know that their ideas have been heard; then they can set goals for their own collaborative skills.

I also really liked the [dialogue]. I would have liked to participate a bit more, I saw myself being shy towards the beginning of the seminar, because I really like getting my ideas out there to people. I also enjoy getting other people's says in different topics that I might not have thought of. For example, when my group was in the seminar, we got a bit off topic and started talking about funding to NASA instead of the Space Race itself. I thought this was actually better for us because we were able to talk about what we wanted to.

GRADING THE REFLECTION

The process of reflection can be a challenge for students, especially if it has not been an established routine in their school lives, but guided reflection is important for students and teacher alike. Reflections are very personal in nature; therefore, there is no right or wrong answer. The goal is for students to be entirely honest in their thoughts about the book and the MINDful reading experience. Consider grading the reflections based on the level of thought that students put into their writing and how they incorporate elements of their reading and discussion of the text. A sample rubric for assessing students' reflections appears on the next page.

Student Feedback

Since students will already have reflected on their experience, collect some student feedback as you read their reflections. An additional survey at the end of the unit is a great way to solicit feedback that will inform the planning of future units. For units with student-selected texts, surveys can help you see how individual students felt about specific books. This helps you better understand why certain books were favored over others. When you review the feedback, think about the connection between books and the level of engagement among students. Did some groups work together better than others? Did students who see themselves as stronger readers tend to like a book more than those who don't see themselves as readers? What changes could be made next time to increase engagement among different learners?

Not everyone will like the book choices. Our research on the Space Race unit showed about 20 percent of students disliked their book choice. We have informally observed that this percentage holds true for most units for the first iteration. This was good information because we were able to identify the unpopular books and replace them with new ones, or at least comment about it in book talks the next time to let students know the books were challenging for others. Reluctant readers were also more likely to report that they disliked a book even though their comprehension of the text and participation in discussion was strong. Part of this could be the product of the mind-set of certain students who feel they are not good readers, who don't like to read, and who don't think nonfiction is worthwhile. As the teacher, it is important to reflect on what students did and did not like about a particular book and use that information moving forward. Sometimes, students will say they didn't like a book when they really mean that the content was challenging for them. They might not know or be familiar with the word "rigor," but they often describe rigorous experiences as "challenging."

As educators, we wish we had 100 percent enthusiasm for everything we teach. It would make our job much easier, but it is not a reality. We must be resilient and realistic about how students will respond to a given text. As you read students' responses, think about

92

Reflection Rubric

	THOUGHTFULNESS	GROWTH	CARE
A	Wow! This is a really thoughtful reflection that shares insights about the text and class discussion. I am really impressed!	The reflection includes thoughtful ideas about your experience and how you plan to improve or develop your dialogue skills next time.	The reflection has been carefully edited and there are no mechanical errors.
B	This is a very good reflection that uses evidence from the discussion and text. I would have liked to hear more though.	The reflection includes some thoughts about your experience and how you plan to improve or develop your dialogue skills next time.	The reflection has been edited, but there are a few mechanical errors.
C	This is a good reflection and some evidence from discussion and the text is present, but there is still a lot of vague description.	The reflection includes some thoughts about your experience, but it is not entirely clear how you plan to improve your dialogue skills.	The reflection has mechanical errors that are distracting to the reader.
REDO	This is a vague reflection, and no evidence from discussion or the text is present.	The reflection is either missing or has very limited reflection about your experience and how you plan to improve next time.	The reflection has not been edited.

the potential changes that are needed and then move forward. The process improves with each unit and each school year, and varies with different groups of students. Nurturing adolescent readers can be an unpredictable and tumultuous process, but students become better readers and thinkers even if they insist that they dislike everything.

A survey provides an opportunity for students to give honest feedback about the books. We often reassure students that they do not have to like every book they read, and nonfiction books present new challenges. Students should be encouraged to critique a book, but just saying, "This book is terrible" is not enough. They need to explain what made the book terrible. Was it too challenging? Too dry? Did it not have enough visuals? These are important things for students to identify as they develop as readers. A sample student feedback form that we posted on Google Docs is shown on page 94.

Stretching Beyond the Textbook © 2014 by Lauren K. Francese and Rebecca H. Marsick, Scholastic Teaching Resources

Response to Nonfiction Selection–Grade 8

Respond to the following questions about your nonfiction text.
* Required

This book/selection is written in a style that is clear and interesting. *

○ weak

○ fair

○ strong

The topic, main ideas, or purpose is obvious. *

○ weak

○ fair

○ strong

The details are helpful, informative, and understandable. *

○ weak

○ fair

○ strong

I can connect with the author's thoughts or feelings about the subject. *

○ weak

○ fair

○ strong

This selection helps me understand people and events. *

○ weak

○ fair

○ strong

Overall I rate this nonfiction selection as . . . *

○ weak

○ fair

○ strong

*Reasons for my rating: ***

*Would you recommend this book to a friend? Why or why not? ***

(Submit)

Here are some examples of what students shared about the Space Race unit books:

I also believe that I chose the correct level for a book. Even though the book was hard to digest, I was able to understand what was happening fairly easily if I read slow enough. In other words, it was tedious, not difficult.

I think that I chose the right level of reading because I was able to understand the story while at the same time, I had to think about it. It was the appropriate amount of challenge and thinking. The best part . . . was actually when we didn't agree on something. This led to a deep and thoughtful discussion. I could take much more out of it then if we agreed on everything which is the worst part. No one really gets much out of a discussion that takes 5 minutes. Next time, I would like to come up with more questions. . . . This will enhance my experience because the meeting will be more effective towards the book.

The only bad part about this experience was that my book was way too easy. One way I could enhance my experience next time would to be choose a more challenging book. The book I chose was really easy to understand and had tons of facts about the Space Race. It didn't occur to me that the book would be so easy during the book talks.

● ● ● ● ●

From the whole-class dialogue, amazing things grow. As content-area teachers, we need to provide another model instead of "Here's the question, and there's the answer" in our classes. The dialogue should evolve in a way so students leave without clear answers. They should exit the room still talking about the discussion questions or stay after to ask more questions. Truth seeking is a tough business. Students need to learn that an open mind and a respect for others' thinking are essential components to being a good student, thinker, and citizen.

Stretching Beyond the Textbook © 2014 by Lauren K. Francese and Rebecca H. Marsick, Scholastic Teaching Resources

CHAPTER 6

Collaboration Leads to Interdisciplinary Connections

> *Tell me and I forget, teach me and I may remember, involve me and I learn.*
>
> —*Ben Franklin*

U sing a variety of nonfiction texts in the content areas will open doors for more interdisciplinary connections, and this will lead to more collaboration and deeper integration of a variety of content areas. Developing a MINDful unit in one classroom is a rich experience on its own, but the more opportunities teachers have to work together, the greater the impact for students.

What Collaboration Means for Teachers

As teachers at both the middle and high school levels, we have been spectators and players in the collaboration game. It's very easy to tell teachers to collaborate, but the reality can be much more complicated. Each content area has curriculum goals, interests, and priorities. Often, teachers end up coordinating instead of collaborating. This is when teachers are teaching related content in separate subject areas, but the material isn't integrated between classrooms. Finding a connection between your content and that of another teacher's can be a difficult task to achieve, but true collaboration is possible with the right attitude.

Our own collaboration began when we found ourselves placed together on a team. We began to work together on interdisciplinary units and aligned themes and topics in our curriculum. But one experience really changed us. We had the opportunity to attend a think tank at Columbia Teachers College, where we spent a day listening to speakers talk about 21st-century learning, collaboration, philosophy of education, and other topics that fascinated us. We returned to school with a new sense of what we wanted to accomplish as teachers. We started planning together and collaborating to find ways to make our classrooms spaces for cross-disciplinary collaboration between and among *our students*. We realized that while *we* worked together, it wasn't clear whether our students were experiencing this, too, or whether they were receiving information that reflected and modeled collaboration.

Coordination and collaboration look different. For example, in our coordination days, Lauren taught about the Jim Crow era in social studies, while Rebecca taught *To Kill a Mockingbird*. Rebecca also discussed the Langston Hughes poem "A Dream Deferred," while Lauren talked about King's "I Have a Dream" speech. But our collaborative work today looks different. Now, we ground our work in the focus question. For example, in our Lincoln unit we both used the focus question: *What does it mean to be free?* We implement the same instruction but add complex texts about Lincoln that students in both classes read. In Lauren's social studies class, the emphasis is on understanding emancipation. In Rebecca's English class, it is on how characters, historical figures, and artists feel about freedom. Even though students are with different classmates in their ELA class and social students classes, they are able to engage in a cross-curricular dialogue with their peers in both classes. A dialogue occurs among students both in and between classrooms, and our collaboration creates an atmosphere in which kids see connections, not between "the stuff we are learning" in the classes, but rather the ideas and thinking taking place between content areas.

Teacher Expertise

When you enter the collaborative process with other teachers, think about who you are as a teacher first. If collaboration means giving up parts of what makes you an effective teacher at the expense of fitting in interdisciplinary work, you will be disappointed in the outcome. Bring your expertise and enthusiasm to the table and share it with others. Take the time to read a book on the content that you want to work on with your colleagues, and discuss it together. Be social about your collaboration and planning. The most successful collaborative teams (both inter-departmental and cross-departmental) are the ones that find friendship within this professional space. We both feel lucky to have collaborators and friends around us as we do our job every day. It does not come without conflict, but how can we ask students to be collaborators when we can't work things out ourselves? Be true to your passions and strengths, and enthusiastically acknowledge them in others, and beautiful things will happen in classrooms throughout your school.

Stretching Beyond the Textbook © 2014 by Lauren K. Francese and Rebecca H. Marsick, Scholastic Teaching Resources

Getting the Work Done

As warm and fuzzy as we can be about the spirit of collaboration, we also know that work just has to get done! Divide the workload with your collaborators. We have given joint assessments and shared the grading. We have held discussions and mini-lessons with our entire team. When we started the Space Race unit, students launched foam rockets in the cafeteria with the science teacher who made the rockets and designed the accompanying "forces in motion" activity. He was so excited, and this enthusiasm transferred to students when it came time to think about which book about the Space Race they were going to read.

We all have different likes and dislikes when it comes to curriculum. Lauren's interest in the Space Race is entirely motivated by her study of the Mercury 13 women, but the truth is, not all kids share that interest. Rebecca loves *To Kill a Mockingbird*, but most kids look at her like she's crazy when she reenacts scenes from the book while standing on a desk. We know that our personal interests seep into our teaching, and they should. Bring this passion to the collaborative process, too. Rebecca might not be as excited about the Space Race as Lauren is, so for this unit she supports Lauren by teaching reading strategies and annotation lessons. For *To Kill a Mockingbird*, Lauren brings the relevant background knowledge and supplemental materials into the unit. When you choose a focus question and ground your planning in a theme, an individual teacher can still retain his or her autonomy and excitement.

THE MIDDLE SCHOOL TEAMING MODEL

Like many middle schools across the country, ours uses a team approach for organizing students. There are different ways that schools can approach teaming, but the one we followed is the one in which teachers across the four core subject areas—social studies, math, science, and ELA—share one group of students. Other approaches to teaming may include a world language teacher or adding a reading teacher and writing teacher to have five core teachers. In any of these scenarios, the greatest benefit is that teachers have a common understanding of shared students. Models like this, in which core teachers share the same group of students, enable those teachers to support one another in strategies that work best with each student. If we see a student struggling,

98

we have three other opinions about what works and what doesn't with that particular student. Or, if we are having trouble working on specific content with a group of students, we have three other teachers to collaborate with in order to help deliver that content in a new way.

Collaboration Requires Planning

In May 2004, the National Middle Schools Association published a summary of the research on teaming titled "NMSA Research Summary #21: Interdisciplinary Teaming." The summary found that one of the most important aspects of working in a team is giving teachers common planning time. On the most basic level, the NMSA states that this time should be used to plan tests and assignments, as well as to plan and coordinate common activities. Teachers should use this planning time to work on interdisciplinary collaboration, too. However, this article cites Jackson & Davis (2000), who claim that, "Teachers' shared time should not come at the expense of their individual planning time. When common planning supplants individual time, collaborative work suffers because teachers are concerned with their own workloads." We have found that the best way to begin to collaborate is to come to a planning meeting with questions about how the other teacher (or teachers) can help supplement and enrich something that's already planned in our specific subject area. Again, there needs to be a shared sense of respect for this to be a smooth process. Sometimes, a few teachers will come to a meeting with ideas, and we have to work out how and where we can help one another with curriculum integration. We have to look at the scope of our individual curricula and see how we can move things around in order to aid one another. However, this is a fantastic problem to have, because it means that everyone is thinking about how to work together for the benefit of students. Remember, not every idea will turn into a fantastic collaborative unit, and that is okay.

We were lucky that our classrooms shared a door. This enables impromptu planning sessions. We constantly discuss what we are teaching each day, as well as in each unit, in order to find a natural connection. If teachers try and force collaboration, due to a school or board initiative, it will not work. Students will see that there is not a fluid connection between the subjects, and therefore, the information will not transfer from one subject area to the other. The ultimate goal of an interdisciplinary collaboration is for students to be learning multiple perspectives on a topic as well as having specific skills reinforced in different classes. We want our students to view the content and skills that we teach as relevant outside the classroom, rather than just something that is subject-specific and test-driven. When students begin to naturally transfer skills from one subject area to another, that is when we know true learning is taking place.

When meeting with colleagues, it's really important to come with an agenda and your own materials. These can include books, lesson plans, curriculum maps, articles, videos, or anything that you might use in planning a lesson or unit. Spend time thinking about what you can do to enhance the unit as well as what you hope your colleagues can do to help you. Collaboration should be a partnership that enhances students' learning opportunities. We would not be the teachers we are today without the ability to borrow ideas from one another.

99

THE HIGH SCHOOL MODEL

The schedule in a traditional high school model can thwart the process of cross-disciplinary collaboration. Teachers are often assigned multiple preparation periods for various grade levels and courses. This limits the ability to find common planning time, but this is not an excuse to teach in a bubble. High school students are still developing reading skills, and they, too, need reading instruction in the content areas. To be honest, this model is perfect for high school because the interdisciplinary elements for a MIND unit can be addressed far more broadly.

While it is often a challenge to get an entire high school department to choose a book or a set of books, it is reasonable to ask each teacher to design a MIND unit that works for him or her. That means all students will be reading a book in social studies around the same time. Then the ELA teachers can incorporate themes, strategy-based instruction, and reflection in their classes in which students use their social studies books. It's all about flexibility. In another example, students read books in Lauren's social studies class for certain units and don't necessarily do anything with them in Rebecca's class because she is working on something else in her curriculum. But at the end of each marking period, Rebecca has students complete a quarterly reading paper. Students have a guided format to share and reflect on a text they read that quarter. Many students take this opportunity to share what they have read in social studies. For this type of experience, we (the teachers) have very little collaboration; it is our students' sense of collaboration between the subjects that creates the connection.

Enhancing Curriculum With the CCSS

With the CCSS advocating for including more complex texts and more informational texts throughout the curriculum, high school departments need to think about how each department can incorporate nonfiction reading in a meaningful way for students. Does this mean holding 100 interdepartmental meetings? Please, no! Does it mean schedules need to change? Probably not. What it does mean is that as teachers begin to incorporate more nonfiction reading, they need to recognize the connections that can be forged between and among students (and even colleagues) as a result of an engaging reading experience.

Adding a large quantity of reading to the already content-heavy curriculum of social studies and science can seem daunting, but this is where teachers need to shift their thinking. Instead of thinking that books and articles are *additional* materials, they should be looking at these new texts as ways to further enhance what they are already doing.

Using the MIND model is a great place to collaborate with an ELA teacher. Work together to find books and articles that will engage students. The ELA teacher can help work on the skills and strategies that are essential to reading nonfiction texts in his or her classroom, as well as provide materials and ideas for teaching these skills within the context of a content-area classroom.

Focus Questions: The Root of Collaboration

In Chapter 3, we discussed the importance of focus questions for student learning. In addition to allowing students to have a common dialogue while reading, focus questions allow teachers to have a common dialogue while collaborating. We have found that one of the ways to approach cross-curricular teaching is through developing these types of questions. Focus questions are a foundation for connecting the curriculum across content areas, thereby helping teachers collaborate. Start with a focus question and see how it can support the deepening of your curriculum as well as that of your colleagues. As Tomlinson and McTighe state in *Integrating Differentiated Instruction and Understanding by Design*, "Questions of this sort are meant to stimulate student thinking about the *reasons* for the content, leading to a deeper understanding of its import" (2006, p. 111). When students internalize reasons for learning content, they are more apt to transfer their knowledge to new situations. And, if students can have multiple experiences across many content areas in which they can transfer their thinking, they will become deeper and more powerful thinkers and learners.

Focus questions that relate to content, skills, and processes should help students uncover the larger purpose of learning the skill. Instead of just being presented a new skill and drilled on it for a test, students should understand *why* the skill is important within the context of their learning. Focus questions surrounding skills and processes are most commonly found in ELA and math classrooms, while questions concerning content are more often found in social studies and science classrooms. Accepting the difference in the type of focus question for certain subject areas can create a good balance when planning an interdisciplinary collaboration.

Again, spend time with your own curriculum first, looking at what the most appropriate focus questions are for your own classroom. Once you've developed your focus questions, come together to see which areas naturally lend themselves to collaboration. Each teacher may have questions and activities that are content specific, but a common focus will allow everyone's students to see bigger connections. Here are some sample focus questions from our Lincoln unit.

Sample Focus Question: What does it mean to be free?

CONTENT-SPECIFIC QUESTIONS

Language Arts:
What is emancipation?
Students explore this concept while they read short stories about slavery.

Social Studies:
Why was Lincoln called "the great emancipator"? Did he deserve the title?
Students explore this concept through reading their Lincoln biographies and the Emancipation Proclamation.

Science:
How do our genetics impact our ability to be free?
Students study genetic diseases (including the possibility of Lincoln's having Marfan syndrome) and explore how they impact freedom.

Focus questions are also the perfect starting point for MINDful reading discussions. As much as we want to find books that touch on the content we're covering in class, it is just as important (and sometimes easier) to focus on books that fall under the same theme or focus question. For example, in a social studies class, if we want students to think about their role as global citizens, we can pull books about different teens around the world who have made a difference in their communities. The connected focus question in ELA could be: *How do the details an author chooses to include help tell the story?* In social studies, the focus question could be: *What are the responsibilities and characteristics of a global citizen?* With the focus in social studies on global citizenship, students can read a variety of books that share this theme, all with different content and reading levels. The ELA teacher can use the idea of craft (an author's choice of specific details) to help support the reading experience. By doing this, students will be learning about all kinds of global citizens in addition to acquiring a new reading strategy.

Analyzing Craft and Structure Across the Curriculum

ENGLISH LANGUAGE ARTS (ELA)	HISTORY, SOCIAL STUDIES	SCIENCE AND TECHNICAL SUBJECTS
• Understand the meaning, tone, and figurative, connotative, and technical meanings • Analyze the structure of specific parts of a text and compare it with other texts • Determine an author's point of view	• Understand and analyze content-specific vocabulary • Identify text structures • Analyze author's point of view and purpose	• Understand symbols, key terms, and other domain-specific vocabulary • Identify text structures • Analyze the author's purpose in providing an explanation, describing a procedure, or discussing an experiment in a text

The ELA teacher can have students use their social studies book to study the various methods an author uses to include the relevant details that tell the story. This allows students to:

■ apply specific reading skills to the use of details in nonfiction text.

■ see how a text can cross disciplines.

■ recognize that their teachers are working together and feel an increased sense of accountability.

■ understand the text from two different perspectives—content and author's craft.

The focus questions have provided the necessary platform for collaboration, and ultimately, deeper student understanding of the content and purpose behind the text.

Backwards Design

In *Understanding by Design,* Wiggins and McTighe incorporate the instructional method of backwards design into writing curriculum. This process is a great way to begin a collaborative approach to interdisciplinary units focused on text discussion. There are three stages to backwards design:

Stage 1: Desired Results

This first stage involves determining what you want students to gain from your unit. Think about the content as well as the skills and strategies you want them to learn. Ultimately, what outcome are you looking for your students to achieve at the completion of this unit?

103

When meeting to discuss their approach reading books in social studies, look at the goals, understanding, and knowledge that you want students to come to through the reading of these texts. Based on what you decide, develop focus questions for these ideas.

In collaboration, each teacher needs to think about the skills and content that must be covered for our particular curriculum area. Then teachers come together and see where there is an overlap. In a collaboration where book discussions are occurring in social studies, the ELA teacher looks at the content that the social studies teacher wants to deliver. Then the ELA teacher decides which reading comprehension skills best fit the types of books he or she wants to use, as well as the students who are in his or her classes.

Stage 2: Assessment Evidence

For this second stage, you must determine how you are going to use formative and summative assessments to drive your instruction. What kind of preassessments do you need to give? Should they be formal or informal, like a classroom observation? How will you use the results of these assessments to help you plan your unit?

Once you have determined *what* you want students to come out of the book discussions knowing and understanding, determine *how* to assess whether this learning has actually occurred. Assessments can be formal, like a paper or a test, but they can also be informal. The book discussions themselves often serve as the best evidence as to what students are gleaning from the text and one another.

ELA teachers often have many models for assessing students' comprehension of text. Therefore, they can work with other content-area teachers to incorporate some of these methods of assessment into their classrooms. Since students have practiced these types of assessments in the ELA classroom, this familiarity allows them to show what they know rather than being confused about the assessment itself. Content-area teachers can get to the content of the books more easily, rather than being unsure about whether students are struggling with reading comprehension or the actual content of the text.

Stage 3: Learning Plan

Stage 3 involves taking the information from stages 1 and 2 and determining the best method of instruction. Couple the ideas of what you want to teach with the knowledge you have gained from assessments to plan your unit.

Once you know the *what* and the *how* of assessing students, figure out the best way to deliver the content and the skills so that students will be engaged in both the text and their discussions with one another.

Establishing a Common Language

Finally, an essential component to collaboration is establishing a common language. If you discuss a reading strategy in ELA, then all the other teachers on the team need to use the same language in their classrooms. Therefore, some of the initial planning time between teachers must be allocated for discussing subject-specific vocabulary. For example, your definition of focus questions must be the same, and you must use these questions in the same manner. Find a language that works for everyone involved and stick to it. Students will notice, and the classroom culture you create will be extended across the content areas.

A SAMPLE ELA-SOCIAL STUDIES UNIT: A CIVIL RIGHTS UNIT

We love to work with all of our colleagues across content areas, but sometimes, given scheduling and time constraints, it is only possible for us to work with each other. The following unit is an example of how we integrated teaching *To Kill a Mockingbird* and civil rights through the focus question: *What does it mean to be a strong leader?*

When we began planning a cross-curricular unit for civil rights, we developed the focus question. We looked at the social studies content that students had to learn and then at the skills and processes they were learning in ELA. In this collaboration, Rebecca's job, as the ELA teacher, was to find the appropriate skills that Lauren could reinforce in her social studies classroom through the content. Lauren's job was to work with Rebecca in planning activities that would build upon the skills and processes that would be taught in the ELA class.

Through joint planning sessions, we structured our calendar so that during the civil rights unit in social studies, language arts classes were reading *To Kill a Mockingbird*. We had two different purposes for teaching this text in each class, but they dovetailed in order to help students come to a greater understanding of both the novel as well as the civil rights movement.

In ELA class, we looked at the role of the narrator in the novel, especially targeting the focus question: *How does our perspective influence the way we see the world?* The ELA discussions were based on the role of Scout, the young narrator, and how her youth and the setting helped shape the events in the story. In addition, to link back to the broader focus question, *What does it mean to be a strong leader?*, we compared Scout's perspective to that of the other characters to determine the ways in which certain characters were successful leaders.

In social studies, students were thinking about the following focus questions:

- *What is the role of the individual in the struggle for civil rights? What is the role of the group?*

- *Can young people make a difference?*

- *What was the role of nonviolent protest during the modern civil rights movement?*

- *Why was strong leadership so significant in creating change?*

All these questions also apply to the content of *To Kill a Mockingbird*. When we sat down together, Lauren described these focus questions and what she wanted students to ultimately understand about the civil rights movement. We recognized that focusing in social studies on the role of the individual and young people directly related to the idea of the narrator's role and perspective that would be discussed in ELA. Therefore, when Lauren taught the book *Claudette Colvin: Twice Toward Justice* in her social studies classroom, she was able to use the same processes for discussing the role of the narrator and how Colvin's voice was used.

105

A SAMPLE ELA-SOCIAL STUDIES UNIT: *HIROSHIMA* (WORLD WAR II UNIT)

The following is an example of how we taught the strategy of annotation between social studies and ELA classes. We have found that annotation is a strategy that many of our students tend to struggle with; therefore, it needs a lot of reinforcement.

Because *Hiroshima* is a complex text, we knew it would be essential for students to annotate it in order to deepen their understanding of the content. In ELA, students learned about the role of annotation and metacognition. One key difference between strong readers and struggling readers is that struggling readers do not recognize when they are missing information. They read until they are finished with the assigned pages and never stop to think if they have actually understood what they have read. Annotation is a way to slow readers down and enable them to be more metacognitive.

We ask students to make the following annotations:

- Questions they have
- Sections of text that surprise them
- Shifts in mood and/or tone
- Strong language
- Important descriptions
- Examples that support the focus questions
- Answers to previously asked questions
- Character development
- Theme
- Author's purpose

Students applied the annotation strategies to their reading of the first chapter of *Hiroshima*.

DAY 1: BOTH CLASSES

We used both a social studies and an ELA period for this activity. Students read and annotated the first chapter of *Hiroshima* for one period, regardless of which class they were in; in the second period (either SS or ELA), they took a multiple-choice quiz on the chapter. They were allowed to use the text and their annotations to help them. This quiz served two purposes:

- Since it was early in the year, it helped us differentiate reading levels.
- It supported discussion with students about the power of annotations after they received their scores.

DAY 2: ELA

In Rebecca's ELA class, students used their quiz on *Hiroshima* and looked at the questions again. Then they reannotated their assigned chapter in red. The goal was to find the answers to the questions they missed and reannotate those sections of the text.

After students reannotated the text, the class discussed how each question required a different kind of metacognitive skill, focusing on fact, inference, and perspective. After showing students which kind of thinking each question required, students marked each kind of question that they got right and wrong on the quiz. Finally, students looked to see if there was a kind of question they missed the most.

In the last part of this ELA lesson, students use their annotations to answer the questions that they got wrong. After showing the correct answers for the entire quiz, students compared their first round of annotations to the ones they marked in red. What did that comparison reveal? Did they read closely enough the first time? How did they think they could improve their annotating and close reading skills for the rest of the text? The class concluded with self-reflection.

DAY 3: SOCIAL STUDIES

Now that students had been through the first chapter of *Hiroshima* and knew what they needed to look for while annotating, they completed a reflection on the preassessment, to determine their challenge level for this book in Lauren's social studies class. Even though all students were reading the same book, we differentiated the assignments to ease the complexity of the multiple perspectives for students.

Students reading at a level 1 (low) focused on one perspective, level 2 (middle) focused on two perspectives, and the level 3 students (high) looked at all six perspectives. This way, all students were able to read the same text and learn the same content, but they accessed it at differing levels of challenge.

As they read, students completed a chart related to their level (see *Hiroshima* differentiated assignments, pages 153–155). They were also given a *Hiroshima* Characters Bookmark (see page 152) to help them keep track of the various characters throughout the text. This is a very helpful tool, especially when students encounter characters with difficult names and have to remember important information that they need to have access to while they read.

A Note About Our Collaborative Process for the *Hiroshima* (World War II) Unit

For our unit on *Hiroshima*, we worked together to determine the goals and objectives for reading this text. Using the Common Core State Standards, we developed our focus questions and then decided upon the best reading strategies to teach in order to help students gain the deepest understanding of the book.

We then looked at the skills and strategies to teach through this text and decided which ones were most appropriate for each subject area. Since students were reading the book in social studies, it made sense that the background knowledge and specific assignment for the book be discussed in that class. ELA tackled the specific skills and strategies for deepening reading comprehension.

Collaborating With Yourself

As we said earlier, we feel very lucky that we have the collaborative model of teaming in our school, but we know that in many schools, teachers do not have this luxury. If you are working alone on your curriculum—be it ELA, social studies, or another content area—you can still use many of the strategies in this chapter to create meaningful book discussions in your classroom.

Make sure to look at the following when you plan a unit, whether you are using one whole-class text or a group of books related by theme:

- Determine the focus questions for the discussion.

- Use backwards design to make sure your desired results are clear. Your assessments will help you determine if those desired results are being met, and this knowledge will allow you to deliver the content in a clear and engaging manner.

- Look at how you can align specific reading comprehension skills with the text or texts that you have chosen.

- Determine how you can use the texts to deliver specific, thematic content.

- If possible, carve out time to go over your plan with a colleague. Even if this is someone who teaches a completely different subject, another teacher's feedback is often invaluable in determining the strengths and weaknesses of a unit.

If you can find just one person in your school to share ideas with, you will feel the impact of collaboration. Find someone you respect as a strong teacher, and he or she will be able to help you with the structure of your unit. Often, just talking about a unit with a colleague will help you better evaluate its design.

●　●　●　●　●

When it's done right, interdisciplinary collaboration is challenging and rigorous work for a teacher. It is never easy to go outside the comfort zone of a classroom with content and strategies that have become a manageable routine. With of the CCSS and the important skills required for the 21st century, students need teachers to create opportunities for cross-curricular work in order to foster a rich learning experience that permeates the walls of classrooms.

CHAPTER 7

21st-Century Learning: Nurturing Adolescent Readers

A capacity, and taste, for reading, gives access to whatever has already been discovered by others. It is the key, or one of the keys, to the already solved problems. And not only so. It gives a relish, and facility, for successfully pursuing the [yet] unsolved ones.

— Abraham Lincoln

With the advent of the CCSS, the discussion about preparing students for the demands of the 21st century has heightened. There is no doubt that students today will need different skills than those of previous generations in order to compete in a globalized world. However, the human condition and the developmental needs of adolescents have not changed as dramatically as the world has. It is important to keep in mind that the students in our classrooms need effective instruction that will give them the tools they need not only to access complex texts but also complex *tasks*.

In his stages of psychosocial development, Erik Erikson theorized that at stage 5, ages 12–18, adolescents seek "clarification of self-identity, life goals and life's meaning." (Corey, p. 63). The questions adolescents ask at this stage are: *Who am I? What are my feelings, attitudes, and beliefs?* Students of this age need to be engaged in deep reading and thinking, and also problem solving. Incorporating a reading experience within project-based learning initiatives deepens and

Stretching Beyond the Textbook © 2014 by Lauren K. Francese and Rebecca H. Marsick, Scholastic Teaching Resources

enriches students' ability to analyze and evaluate within larger learning initiatives and cross-disciplinary work.

Deliberate Practice

Using MINDful reading in your classroom will give students opportunities to develop their talents as readers. Being a talented reader is not necessarily a natural gift, but rather a skill that requires practice and persistence. While many other commonly used reading strategies involve repetition, MINDful reading provides flexibility for teachers to incorporate targeted reading instruction (practice) for groups of learners through a differentiated process. This process makes the reading experience more fluid, and more flexible, within a variety of tasks.

In recent years, there has been a surge in "success literature," which has been extensively published and marketed to professionals in the corporate world. Some of that research has focused on how talent is developed, where it comes from, and why it is present in some individuals and not others. Much of this research comes from K. Anders Ericsson, a Swedish psychologist and professor of psychology at the University of Florida, and his colleagues who have been cited extensively. While their research shows examples in a variety of fields, the relevance to education and literacy instruction shines through, and their research yields some interesting results pertaining to literacy instruction. What stands out most is the concept of "deliberate practice." When educators (and others) think about practice, we often think about repetition, but Ericsson and his colleagues make an important distinction about practice. They note, "Deliberate practice includes activities that have been specially designed to improve the current level of performance" (1993, p. 368). This makes a good case for differentiated tasks, books at a variety of reading levels, and instruction in nonfiction reading strategies. They also identify the following conditions for improving performance:

- "... the subjects' motivation to attend to the task and exert effort to improve their performance."

- "... the design of the task should take into account the preexisting knowledge of the learners so that the task can be correctly understood after a brief period of instruction."

- "The subjects should receive immediate informative feedback and knowledge of results of their performance."

- "The subjects should repeatedly perform the same or similar tasks. . . . In the absence of adequate feedback, efficient learning is impossible and improvement only minimal even for highly motivated subjects. Hence, mere repetition of an activity will not automatically lead to improvement in, especially, accuracy of performance (Trowbridge & Cason, 1932)." (p. 367)

Motivation, background knowledge, and ongoing feedback are major contributors to improving students' performance. Reading nonfiction texts in the content areas places students in an environment that supports these factors. Reading and engaging in a

110

meaningful dialogue about text provides deliberate practice in reading effectively for the real world. Ericsson, et al. also note that ". . . deliberate practice is a highly structured activity, the explicit goal of which is to improve performance. Specific tasks are invented to overcome weaknesses, and performance is carefully monitored to provide cues for ways to improve it further" (p. 368). As much as the theory of deliberate practice is applicable in the professional world, it is also fitting that this be applied to literacy instruction.

About 21st-Century Skills

The Partnership for 21st Century Skills publishes a toolkit for teachers that notes the alignment of 21st-century skills and the CCSS. It states:

- *The CCSS explicitly call for, and integrate, **higher-order thinking skills** as a means to achieving career and college readiness for all students.*

- *The CCSS have established **widespread consensus** around a national baseline for college and career readiness which includes a focus on rigorous core academic content mastery along with competencies like critical thinking, reasoning, communication and collaboration (p. 4)*

CRITICAL THINKING AND REASONING

MIND units are easily adapted to foster critical thinking skills. The design of focus questions is essential here. Establishing a focus question and anchoring a unit in thematic questions will guide students to think deeply about the text. In the content areas, teachers often use "essential questions" and "research questions" to guide projects. Shifting to a thematic approach for instruction throughout an entire unit will allow students time to preview and think about a question over an extended period of time. When they enter a project-based task, it is a cognitive challenge to absorb the content and questions all at once. Integrating nonfiction text through a MIND experience provides students with the opportunity to enter a project with depth and clarity about a topic.

With an emphasis on research skills in the CCSS, the design of research-based tasks will require more attention across subject areas. Students need to develop as nonfiction readers in order to effectively manage the research process and incorporate their findings into projects and written work. Successful researchers *are* effective nonfiction readers. Consider spending time on deep reading and thinking in connection with project-based tasks. For example, the Lincoln unit we shared in previous chapters did not end when the books did. Afterward, students continued exploring the focus question: *What does it mean to be free?* Students visited a local museum to see an exhibit on the Emancipation Proclamation and the legacy of slavery in their own community. After all of this deep thinking about the content, they worked in groups to research issues affecting their freedom and wrote their own documents and speeches explaining what freedoms young people in America and around the world should have that they don't. The emergence of critical thinking for this project was much more natural for students because they had spent a good amount of time thinking about the question from other angles before the project began.

COMMUNICATION AND COLLABORATION

Students who struggle with communication can often find the small-group meetings and dialogue challenging. Not every student has the confidence or ability to take a leading role in a discussion with his or her peers. As teachers, we do everything we can to support students as they search for the confidence and competence to communicate with others.

The Speaking and Listening components of the CCSS outline the development of collaboration skills for students. The whole-class dialogue is often a real test of these skills. It's very common for students to write in their reflections that they wish they'd shared more, or to say, "I want to talk more next time to get a better grade." This is always interesting because students are graded not only on their contributions (speaking), but also on their active engagement with the ideas of others (listening) throughout the process. Students who "steamroll" their classmates in small-group meetings and the whole-class dialogue do not (and should not) receive a score of exemplary (A range) for speaking and listening. As part of the collaborative process in their groups and the dialogue, students begin to develop a balance between the skills of speaking and listening.

One day, a student came to Lauren's social studies class with a detailed organizer. He had outlined his ideas in numerical scales from 0–10 on the organizer as his way of "counting" the level of each individual's perspective throughout the book. As the dialogue unfolded and he shared his numbers, his classmates stared, perplexed. They had no idea what he was saying. Since there's always time within the dialogue for students to provide feedback, his classmates (very appropriately) shared that he was not communicating effectively. After class, the student discussed his scales with Lauren and revealed that he saw the world in numbers, but he had never quite thought about the fact that other people might not see things in the same way. This was a very important realization for this student, and he went on to rethink his approach to the dialogue and other group work. By the end of the school year, his self-awareness and ability to share his thinking with others showed significant improvement.

Through the process of MINDful reading experiences, teachers and students have opportunities to be reflective and work together to accomplish a variety of goals. Sometimes, a student is an exceptional reader but a poor communicator. These students soar through the reading and thinking about nonfiction text but struggle to share with others. In contrast, there are students who really struggle to access complex nonfiction text but who are highly effective communicators. These students work to develop reading skills through the process and shine in the culminating dialogue.

Stretching Beyond the Textbook © 2014 by Lauren K. Francese and Rebecca H. Marsick, Scholastic Teaching Resources

Project-Based Learning

The MIND model can be embedded into the project-based learning model in a variety of ways. Here are a few suggestions for meaningful ways to bring MINDful work to project-based tasks:

- When giving students a real-world problem to solve, consider using authentic texts. Professional texts such as handbooks and other literature will give the task authenticity and help students see what nonfiction text looks like in the adult world. Use the strategies in this book to help students persist in reading and gaining understanding of these authentic texts.

- Bring in content-area experts—teachers, doctors, lawyers, businesspeople, authors, and so on—to help students understand the topic. Ask the expert to present to your students as if he or she were presenting to colleagues. Use the Shopping in a Text strategy (page 76) or Why Do You Think That? Organizer (page 126) during the presentation so students can practice these skills as they view the presentation.

- Use biographical texts as a way of launching a project in which students may need to take on a role. For example, the science teacher we work with has students choose a biography of a famous scientist before they begin research for their science fair projects. He has developed a MIND unit specifically focused on what scientists do, how they research, and who they are as real people.

● ● ● ● ●

Through the process of planning, instructing, and reflecting on the 21st-century classroom, it becomes clear that access to complex and authentic nonfiction texts will allow students to develop the skills that will be required in the real world. Developing MINDful reading experiences for students provides both the depth of content and the support for essential reading skills. We cannot accomplish this in our classrooms unless we stretch beyond our textbooks and consider the possibilities of meaningful, interdisciplinary units that create opportunities for reading rich nonfiction and engaging in thoughtful dialogue.

Stretching Beyond the Textbook © 2014 by Lauren K. Francese and Rebecca H. Marsick, Scholastic Teaching Resources

References

LITERATURE CITED

Ahmedi, F. (2005). *The other side of the sky: A memoir*. New York: Simon and Schuster.

Ali, N., & Minoui, D. (2012). *I am Nujood, Age 10 and divorced*. New York: Three Rivers Press.

Bartoletti, S. C. (2010). *They called themselves the KKK*. New York: Houghton Mifflin.

Beah, I. (2007). *A long way gone: Memoirs of a boy soldier*. New York: Farrar, Straus and Giroux.

Boo, K. (2012). *Behind the beautiful forevers*. New York: Random House.

Carson, C. (Ed.). (1998). *The autobiography of Martin Luther King, Jr.* New York: Warner Books.

Colbert, D. (2009). *Abraham Lincoln (10 days)*. New York: Aladdin.

Colbert, D. (2008). *Anne Frank (10 days)*. New York: Aladdin.

Colbert, D. (2008). *Martin Luther King, Jr. (10 days)*. New York: Aladdin.

Crowe, C. (2002). *Mississippi trial, 1955*. New York: Penguin Group.

Durrow, H. W. (2010). *The girl who fell from the sky*. Chapel Hill, NC: Algonquin Books.

Elster, J. A. (2008). *Who's Jim Hines?* Detroit: Wayne State University Press.

Fetter-Vorm, J. (2013). *Trinity: A graphic history of the first atomic bomb*. New York: Hill and Wang.

Floca, B. (2009). *Moonshot: The flight of Apollo 11*. New York: Atheneum.

Ford, J. (2009). *House on the corner of Bitter and Sweet*. New York: Random House.

Freedman, R. (1987). *Lincoln: A photobiography*. New York: Houghton Mifflin.

Gantos. J. (2002). *Hole in my life*. New York: Farrar, Straus & Giroux.

Glasscock, S. (2013). John Lewis continues to fight. Unpublished article.

Harden, B. (2012). *Escape from camp 14: One man's remarkable odyssey from North Korea to freedom in the west*. New York: Penguin Group.

Henry. O. (Writer). (1992). *The life and times of Abraham Lincoln* [VHS video]. United States: Delphi Productions.

Hersey, J. (1989). *Hiroshima*. New York: Alfred A. Knopf, Inc.

Hoose, P. (2009). *Claudette Colvin: Twice toward justice*. New York: Farrar, Straus and Giroux.

Hoose, P. (2001). *We were there, too!: Young people in U.S. history*. New York: Farrar, Straus and Giroux.

Houston, J. W., & Houston, J. D. (1973). *Farewell to Manzanar*. New York: Laurel Leaf Books.

Hughes, L. (2001). The black man speaks. *The collected words of Langston Hughes, Vol. 2* (A Rampersad, Ed.). Columbia, MO: The University of Missouri Press.

Kiernan, D. (2013). *The girls of Atomic City: The untold story of the women who helped win World War II*. New York: Simon & Schuster.

Kuklin, S. (2008). *No choirboy*. New York: Henry Holt and Company.

Lee, H. (1960). *To kill a mockingbird*. New York: Harper.

Ling, L., & Ling, L. (2010). *Somewhere inside: One sister's captivity in North Korea and the other's fight to bring her home*. New York: HarperCollins.

McGowen, T. (2008). *Space race: The mission, the men, the moon*. New York: Aladdin.

McCormick. P. (2006). *Sold*. New York: Hyperion.

Mandela, N. (1995). *A long walk to freedom*. New York: Little, Brown and Company.

Mathabane, M. (1986). *Kaffir boy: The true story of a black youth's coming of age in apartheid South Africa*. New York: Touchstone.

Moore, W. (2010). *The other Wes Moore: One name, two fates*. New York: Spiegel & Grau.

Myers, W. D. (1993). *Malcolm X: By any means necessary*. New York: Scholastic.

Myers, W. D. (1999). *Monster*. New York: HarperCollins.

Nolen, S. (2004). *Promised the moon: The untold story of the first women in the space race*. New York: Thunder's Mouth Press.

Opdyke, I. (2004). *In my hands: Memories of a Holocaust rescuer*. New York: Dell Laurel-Leaf.

O'Reilly, B., & Dugard, M. (2011). *Killing Lincoln: The shocking assassination that changed America forever.* New York: Henry Holt and Company.

O'Reilly, B., & Zimmerman, D. J. (2012). *Lincoln's last days: The shocking assassination that changed America forever.* New York: Henry Holt and Company.

Ottavani, J. (2009). *T-Minus: The race to the moon.* New York: Aladdin.

Ottaviani, J. (2001). *Fallout: J. Robert Oppenheimer, Leo Szilard, and the political science of the atomic bomb.* Ann Arbor: Michigan: G.T. Labs.

Reher, K. (Producer), & Sohn, P. (Writer/Director). (2009). *Partly cloudy.* [Animated Short Film] United States: Pixar Animation Studios/Walt Disney Pictures.

Scott, D. & Leonov, A. (2004). *Two sides of the moon: Our story of the Cold War Space Race.* New York: St. Martin's Press.

Sheinkin, S. (2012). *Bomb: The race to build and steal the world's most dangerous weapon.* New York: Roaring Book Press.

Sheinkin, S. (2012). *Lincoln's grave robbers.* New York: Scholastic.

Skrypuch, M. F. (2008). *Daughter of war.* Brighton, MA: Fitzhenry & Whiteside.

St. George, J. (1999). *In the line of fire: presidents' lives at stake.* New York: Holiday House.

Stokes, J. A., Viola, H., & Wolf, L. (2007). *Students on strike: Jim Crow, civil rights, Brown, and me.* Des Moines: IA: National Geographic Children's Books.

Stone, T. (2009). *Almost astronauts: 13 women who dared to dream.* Somerville, MA: Candlewick Press.

Sullivan, G. (2000). *Abraham Lincoln (in his own words).* New York: Scholastic.

Swanson, J. L. (2009). *Chasing Lincoln's killer.* New York: Scholastic.

Swanson, J. L. (2006). *Manhunt: The 12-day chase for Lincoln's killer.* New York: HarperCollins.

Thimmesh, C. (2006). *Team moon: How 400,000 people landed Apollo 11 on the moon.* New York: Houghton Mifflin.

Tyson, N. deGrasse. (2012). *Space chronicles.* New York: W.W. Norton & Company.

Ung, L. (2000). *First they killed my father: A daughter of Cambodia remembers.* New York: HarperCollins.

Vawter, V. (2013). *Paperboy.* New York: Delacorte Press.

Yep, L. (1996). *Hiroshima.* New York: Scholastic.

PROFESSIONAL LITERATURE CITED

Boyle, N. (2012/2013). Closing in on close reading. *Educational Leadership, 70*(4), 36–41.

Calkins, L., Ehrenworth, M., & Lehman, C. (2012). *Pathways to the Common Core: Accelerating achievement.* Portsmouth, NH: Heinemann.

Capalongo-Bernadowski, C. (2007). Book clubs at work. *Library media connection, 26*(3), 32–33.

Coleman, D. Standards for the English class. *NYTimes.com.* Dec. 5, 2012. Retrieved January 3, 2013, from nytimes.com/2012/12/05/opinion/standards-for-english-class.html

Coleman, D., & Pimentel, S. (2012). Revised publishers' criteria for the Common Core State Standards in English Language Arts and Literacy, Grades 3–12. n.p.

Corey, G. (2005). *Theory and practice of counseling and psychotherapy* (7th ed.). Belmont, CA: Brooks/Cole Thompson Learning.

Cunningham, A. E., & Stanovich K. E. (2001). What reading does for the mind. *Journal of Direct Instruction. 1*(2), 137–149.

Daniels, H. (2002, May). Expository text in literature circles. *Voices From the Middle, 9*(4), 7–14.

Daniels, H. (2002). *Literature circles: Voice and choice in book clubs & reading groups.* Portland, ME: Stenhouse.

Day, J. P., Spiegal, D. L., McLellan, J., & Brown, V. B. (2002). *Moving forward with literature circles.* New York: Scholastic.

Ericsson, K. A., Krampe, R. T., & Tesch-Romer, C. (1993). The role of deliberate practice in the acquisition of expert performance. *Psychological Review 100*(3), 363–406.

Friedman, T., If you've got the skills, she's got the job. *NYTimes.com.* Nov. 17, 2012. Retrieved January 10, 2012, from nytimes.com/2012/11/18/opinion/sunday/Friedman-You-Got-the-Skills.html

Gallagher, K. (2009). *Readicide: How schools are killing reading and what you can do about it.* Portland, ME: Stenhouse Publishers.

Gallagher, K. (2004). *Deeper reading: Comprehending challenging texts, 4–12.* Portland, ME: Stenhouse.

How to read a hard book. (n.d). Retrieved October 28, 2013, from oprah.com./omagazine/How-to-Read-a-Hard-Book

International Reading Association. (1999). *On adolescent literacy* [Resolution]. Retrieved October 8, 2010, from reading.org/general/AboutIRA/Resolutions.aspx

Jackson, A. W., & Davis, G. A. (2000). *Turning points 2000: Educating adolescents in the 21st century.* New York: Teachers College Press.

Keene, E.O., & Zimmerman, S. (1997). *Mosaic of thought: Teaching comprehension in a reading workshop.* Portsmouth, NH: Heinemann.

Magner, T., Soulé, H., & Wesolowski, K. (2011). *P21 Common Core guidebook: A guide to aligning the Common Core State Standards with the framework for 21st century skills.* Washington, DC: Partnership for 21st Century Skills.

Matthews, J. Fiction vs. nonfiction smackdown. Retrieved October 18, 2012, from articles.washingtonpost.com/2012-10-17/local/35499782_1_common-core-standards-nonfiction-sandra-stotsky

Mertens, S. B., & Flowers, N. (2004). *Interdisciplinary teaming* (NMSA Research Summary #21). Retrieved June 8, 2013, from www.ncmle.org/researchsummaries/ressum21.html

Minzesheimer, Bob. How the "Oprah Effect" changed publishing. Retrieved May 22, 2011, from usatoday30.usatoday.com/life/books/news/2011-05-22-Oprah-Winfrey-Book-Club_n.htm

Mosle, S. (2002). What should children read and why? Retrieved November 22, 2012, from opinionator.blogs.nytimes.com/2012/11/22/what-should-children-read/?_r=0

National Assessment Governing Board. (2009). Reading framework for the 2009 National Assessment of Educational Progress. Washington, DC: U.S. Government Printing Office.

National Governors Association Center for Best Practices, Council of Chief State School Officers. (2010). *Common core state standards.* Washington D.C: National Governors Association Center for Best Practices, Council of Chief State School Officers.

O'Brien, C. (2007). Using collaborative reading groups to accommodate diverse learning and behavior needs in the general education classroom. *Beyond Behavior, 16*(3), 7–15.

O'Donnell-Allen, C. (2006). *The book club companion.* Portsmouth, NH: Heinemann.

Office of Research and Analysis. (2007). *To read or not to read: A question of national consequence* (Research report: #47). Washington, DC: National Endowment for the Arts.

Office of Research and Analysis. (2009). *Reading on the rise: A new chapter in American literacy.* Washington, DC: National Endowment for the Arts.

Pitcher, S. M., Martinez, G., Dicembre, E. A., Fewster, D., & McCormick, M. K. (2001). The literacy needs of adolescents in their own words. *Journal of Adolescent and Adult Literacy, 53*(8), 636–645.

Ritchhart, R., Church, M., & Morrison, K. (2011). *Making thinking visible.* San Francisco: Jossey-Bass.

Strong, R., Silver, H. F., & Perini, M. J. (2001). *Teaching what matters most: Standards and strategies for raising student achievement.* Alexandria, VA: Association for Supervision and Curriculum Development.

Sullivan S., Nichols, B., Bradshaw, T., & Rogowski, K. (2007). To read or not to read. National Endowment for the Arts Research Report #47. Washington, D.C.

Thompson, G., Madhuri, M., & Taylor, D. (2008). How the Accelerated Reader program can become counterproductive for high school students. *Journal of Adolescent & Adult Literacy, 51*(7), 550–560.

Tomlinson, C. A., & McTighe, J. (2006). *Integrating differentiated instruction and understanding by design.* Alexandria, VA: Association for Supervision and Curriculum Development.

Wiggins, G., & McTighe, J. (2005). *Understanding by design* (2nd ed.). Alexandria, VA: Association for Supervision and Curriculum Development.

Wu, Katie. The book club phenomena. Retrieved February 8, 2011, from mcsweeneys.net/articles/the-book-club-phenomena

Suggested Texts With Lexile Ranges

World War II (or Atomic Bomb) Unit

Whole-Class Text:

Hiroshima by John Hersey (1190L)

Student-Selected Texts:

Bomb: The Race to Build and Steal the World's Most Dangerous Weapon by Steve Sheinkin (920L)

Trinity: A Graphic History of the First Atomic Bomb by Jonathan Fetter-Vorm (GN950L)

Farewell to Manzanar by Jeanne Wakatsuki Houston and James D. Houston (1040L)

Fallout by Jim Ottaviani (1040L)

The Girls of Atomic City: The Untold Stories of the Women Who Helped Win World War II by Denise Kiernan (none listed)

Historical Fiction Options:

House on the Corner of Bitter and Sweet by Jamie Ford (850L)

Hiroshima by Laurence Yep (660L)

Civil Rights Unit

Whole-Class Text:

Claudette Colvin: Twice Toward Justice by Phillip Hoose (1000L)

Student-Selected Texts:

Malcolm X: By Any Means Necessary by Walter Dean Myers (1050L)

Students on Strike: Jim Crow, Civil Rights, Brown, and Me by John A. Stokes, Herman Viola, and Lois Wolf (1030L)

They Called Themselves the KKK by Susan Campbell Bartoletti (1180L)

We Were There, Too! by Phillip Hoose (950L)

Martin Luther King, Jr. (10 Days) by David Colbert (1060L)

The Other Wes Moore: One Name, Two Fates by Wes Moore (990L)

Historical Fiction Pairing:

Who's Jim Hines? by Jean Elster (none listed)

Monster by Walter Dean Myers (670L)

Mississippi Trial, 1955 by Chris Crowe (870L)

The Girl Who Fell From the Sky by Heidi W. Durrow (none listed)

Lincoln Unit

Whole-Class Text:

Lincoln: A Photobiography by Russell Freedman (1040L)

Student-Selected Texts:

Manhunt: The 12-Day Chase for Lincoln's Killer by James L. Swanson (none listed)

Chasing Lincoln's Killer by James L. Swanson (young reader's version) (980L)

Killing Lincoln: The Shocking Assassination That Changed America Forever by Bill O'Reilly and Martin Dugard

Lincoln's Last Days by Bill O'Reilly and Dwight Jon Zimmerman (illustrated version) (1020L)

Abraham Lincoln (10 Days) by David Colbert (NC1110L)

Historical Fiction Pairing:

Lincoln's Grave Robbers by Steve Sheinkin (930L)

Space Race Unit

Whole-Class Text: (2 options)

Team Moon: How 400,000 People Landed Apollo 11 on the Moon by Catherine Thimmesh (1060L)

Almost Astronauts by Tanya Stone (980L)

Student-Selected Texts:

Team Moon: How 400,000 People Landed Apollo 11 on the Moon by Catherine Thimmesh (1060L)

Almost Astronauts by Tanya Stone (980L)

Moonshot: The Flight of Apollo 11 by Brian Floca (990L)

Two Sides of the Moon: Our Story of the Cold War Space Race by David Scott and Alexei Leonov (none listed)

Promised the Moon: The Untold Story of the First Women in the Space Race by Stephanie Nolen (none listed)

The Space Race: The Mission, the Men, the Moon by Tom McGowen (none listed)

Space Chronicles by Neil deGrasse Tyson (none listed)

Historical Fiction Option:

T-Minus: The Race to the Moon by Jim Ottavani (none listed)

Human Rights/Global Studies

Whole-Class Text: (2 options)

I Am Nujood, Age 10 and Divorced by Nujood Ali with Delphine Minoui (none listed)

A Long Way Gone: Memoirs of a Boy Soldier by Ishmael Beah (920L)

Student-Selected Texts:

Anne Frank (10 Days) by David Colbert (980L)

No Choirboy by Susan Kuklin (690L)

Somewhere Inside: One Sister's Captivity in North Korea and the Other's Fight to Bring Her Home by Laura Ling and Lisa Ling (none listed)

Behind the Beautiful Forevers by Katherine Boo (1030L)

Kaffir Boy by Mark Mathabane (1040L)

In My Hands: Memories of a Holocaust Rescuer by Irene Opdyke (890L)

Escape from Camp 14 by Blaine Harden (none listed)

The Other Side of the Sky by Farah Ahmedi (850L)

Historical Fiction Pairing:

Sold by Patricia McCormick (820L)

Daughter of War by Marsha Fochuk Skrypuch (none listed)

You can consult lexile.com to assess the levels of texts for other units. Other good sites to consult for nonfiction texts for adolescents are ala.org/yalsa and goodreads.com.

Why Read Nonfiction Text?

"When I was your age, television was called books."
—William Goldman, *The Princess Bride*

Dear Students,

Reading nonfiction text in social studies is really important for your development as a reader. Nonfiction is the type of text that you will encounter when you enter the professional and "real" world. While it is important to read a wide variety of texts, and fiction is always exciting and important to your development as a student, reader, writer, and human being, nonfiction will be the key to your academic success.

Thomas Friedman recently published an op-ed in *The New York Times* (that's nonfiction, too) about American education. He described an executive running a major steel welding company that was looking for skilled workers and having trouble finding them. The executive finally found the right person for the job, and here is how she described that person: *"'She knows how to read a weld code. She can write work instructions and make sure that the people on the floor can weld to that instruction,' so 'we solved the problem by training our own people,' said Tapani, adding that while schools are trying hard, training your own workers is often the only way for many employers to adapt to 'the quick response time' demanded for 'changing skills.'"*

Did you read that? The business owner is talking about on-the-job training. Do you know what that means? The better you are at understanding nonfiction text (descriptive text, reports, manuals, codes, instructions, and so on), the better you will be able to adapt and train for professions in the future! I can't think of any skilled professions that do not require some nonfiction reading skills. So read on, kids. This skill is what will help you learn, adapt, and grow with the times.

In this classroom, not only do you get to read nonfiction, but you also discuss it with others. This makes the reading experience social. You can talk about the text, ask questions, and complain to each other about how much work you have. Remember that *you* decide how many pages you need to read each night. Misery loves company. In all seriousness, being social while reading is a great way to learn. You have a group of people who can provide support and multiple perspectives throughout the process.

Your dialogue with one another adds a whole other level to the reading experience. Now you will get to hear ALL of your classmates talk about the text (or texts). We will have a discussion in class as a final assessment of the reading experience. You will be scored based on your active participation. If you decide to hide throughout the unit, not fully read your book, or just goof around, this is where the trouble lies. You will be expected to discuss the text using evidence from it. It is a fluid process of trying to develop new wonderings and a better understanding of others, the world, and yourselves. Imagine the things you can learn about yourself and others just by reading, participating, and being prepared.

My expectation is that you will engage in this process in the following ways:

- Read your book.
- Participate in small-group meetings.
- Come to your group and class prepared.
- Communicate what you enjoy and what challenges you.

Best wishes,

Your Teacher

Sample Reading Inventory

Administer a reading inventory two to four times throughout the school year. We suggest that you keep a file for each student and date each inventory. This is a great way to track the changing skill sets and attitudes of your students.

At the end of the year, you can have students look back at their inventories and see the changes in their skills and their attitudes through what they have recorded.

Ask students to write a reflection based on the following three points. They should be looking at their completed Reading Checklist and noting changes that they see in their responses over the course of the year.

- *What changes do you notice in the skills you use as a reader? Complete the "When I read, I" column.*

- *What changes do you notice in your attitude toward reading? Complete the "My reading personality" column.*

- *Please use specific books we read and discussed this year to show evidence of these changes.*

Name _____ Period _____ Date _____

Reading Checklist

Check off all the items that complete each sentence for you, including anything that you might do even *some* of the time.

When I read I:

_____ take notes for academic assignments.

_____ use a highlighter or underline important information.

_____ annotate.

_____ reread passages to ensure understanding.

_____ look up words that I don't know.

_____ find additional information about topics I am unfamiliar with.

_____ use text features to help me (chapter titles, charts, illustrations, captions, maps, sidebars, and so on).

_____ use text structures to help me.

_____ ask questions to clarify understanding.

_____ read different genres.

_____ prefer to read magazines.

My reading personality:

_____ I read for enjoyment; I often choose to read during my free time.

_____ I read if I have to.

_____ I turn off all of my electronics when I sit down to read.

_____ I find a place away from any distractions.

_____ I have a hard time understanding most of what I read.

_____ I understand most all of what I read.

_____ I like to talk about what I read.

_____ I like to recommend books to my friends.

_____ I get recommendations from my parents and teachers.

_____ Reading makes me want to throw up.

_____ I enjoy reading my favorite books over and over again.

Text Structures

Description

The author provides detailed information about a topic, concept, event, person, idea, or object by listing characteristics, features, facts, and details. This includes language that is literal and/or figurative.

WORDS THAT HELP YOU RECOGNIZE DESCRIPTION:

for example	*such as*	*some characteristics are*
look at	*it is like ____*	*look closely, and you'll see . . .*
it is as ____ as ____ (makes a comparison)		

Sequence of Events

Sequence is the chronological (time) order of the events in a text.
The author lists items or events in a specific order.
(How to make or do something is just one example of the sequence text structure.)

WORDS THAT HELP YOU RECOGNIZE A SEQUENCE:

until	*before*	*after*	*next*
finally	*now*	*first/last*	
then	*on (date)*	*at (time)*	

Problem and Solution

The author states a problem and lists one or more potential solutions and their results.

WORDS AND PHRASES THAT HELP YOU RECOGNIZE PROBLEM AND SOLUTION:

one reason is	*a solution*
a problem	*solved by*
outcome is	*issues are*

Stretching Beyond the Textbook © 2014 by Lauren K. Francese and Rebecca H. Marsick, Scholastic Teaching Resources

Compare and Contrast

The author explains how two or more things are alike and/or how they are different.

WORDS THAT HELP YOU RECOGNIZE COMPARE AND CONTRAST:

on the other hand	however	other than	differently
and yet	similar to	like	different from
similarly	but	nevertheless	while
likewise	as opposed to	either . . . or	neither . . . nor
least	most	less than	more than
unlike	difference	same as	not only . . . but also

Cause and Effect

The author describes one or more causes (things that happened) and the resulting effect or effects. This is related to problem and solution, but NO SOLUTION is proposed.

WORDS THAT HELP YOU RECOGNIZE CAUSE AND EFFECT:

since	therefore	this led to	due to
so that	for this reason	consequently	as a result
because	thus	nevertheless	if . . . then
then	so		

123

Name _____ Period _____ Date _____

What's Happening?

Complete the organizer by summarizing what you have read and how it connects to the focus question.

Focus Question: _____

WHAT'S HAPPENING? SUMMARIZE IMPORTANT EVENTS IN THE TEXT.	HOW DOES EACH EVENT CONNECT TO THE FOCUS QUESTION?

124

Stretching Beyond the Textbook © 2014 by Lauren K. Francese and Rebecca H. Marsick, Scholastic Teaching Resources

Name _____ Period _____ Date _____

What's the Big Deal?

After reading, identify three important events from the text. Then explain why they are such a big deal.

IMPORTANT EVENT	WHY IS IT A BIG DEAL?	HOW DOES THIS HELP YOU ANSWER THE FOCUS QUESTION?

Name _____ Period _____ Date _____

Why Do You Think That?

After reading the text, identify three important new things you have learned from the book. Then explain why and how you arrived at that new learning.

NEW LEARNING	WHY DO YOU THINK THAT? USE EVIDENCE (QUOTES) FROM THE TEXT.

Name _____ Period _____ Date _____

What Does the Text Say?
What Do I Have to Say?

After reading, choose three quotes that help you answer, or relate to, the focus question. Then explain your thinking about each quote.

WHAT DOES THE TEXT SAY?	WHAT DO I HAVE TO SAY?

Name _____ Period _____ Date _____

What Makes You Wonder?

Complete the first two columns while you are reading. Be sure to note the page numbers in the text. Complete the last column after discussing your thoughts and questions with your group in class.

QUOTE WITH PAGE #	AFTER READING THIS . . .	MY GROUP DISCUSSED THIS . . .

Stretching Beyond the Textbook © 2014 by Lauren K. Francese and Rebecca H. Marsick, Scholastic Teaching Resources

Name _____ Period _____ Date _____

Sequence of Events

Draw the sequence of events in the section of text you have read.
Write a quote from the text under each drawing.

#1	#4
Quote:	Quote:
#2	#5
Quote:	Quote:
#3	#6
Quote:	Quote:

Stretching Beyond the Textbook © 2014 by Lauren K. Francese and Rebecca H. Marsick, Scholastic Teaching Resources

Name _____ Period _____ Date _____

Multiple Perspectives

Choose three people or groups in the book. Using evidence from the text, explain each perspective as it is presented in the text.

PERSON OR GROUP: Use evidence from the text to write a brief description of each.	PERSPECTIVE: Use evidence from the text and your own thinking to describe the person or group's perspective.

Empathy

WALKING IN ANOTHER'S SHOES

Choose two people or groups from the text and describe what you think they might be feeling and thinking. Use evidence from the book and your own thinking.

PERSON OR GROUP: Explain why you chose this person or group.	EMPATHIZE: How do you think this person or group is feeling? What might this person or group be thinking?

131

Stretching Beyond the Textbook © 2014 by Lauren K. Francese and Rebecca H. Marsick, Scholastic Teaching Resources

Name _____ Period _____ Date _____

Words From the Wise

As you read, identify important words or short phrases. Explain why you feel each is significant to the focus question and overall topic.

WORD OR PHRASE (include page number)	WHY? WHAT MAKES THIS SIGNIFICANT?

132

Samples: Write-to-Think

....

Lincoln Unit Write-to-Think

"It is great folly to attempt to make anything out of me or my early life. It can all be condensed into a simple sentence, and that sentence you will find in Gray's Elegy: 'The short and simple annals of the poor.' That's my life and that's all you or anyone else can make out of it."

Gray's Elegy: written by Thomas Gray, an English poet, completed in 1750 and first published in 1751.

How do you think Lincoln's experience as a child living in poverty shaped him as a person and a leader?

....

Civil Rights Unit Write-to-Think

I swear to the Lord / I still can't see / Why Democracy means / Everybody but me.

—Langston Hughes

What people or groups did democracy not apply to, based on your reading? Do you feel that "Democracy means" you? Why or why not?

....

Space Race Unit Write-to-Think

"I think one of the things we had was a common goal; and we all realized that we were into something that was one of the few things in history that was going to stand out over the years. We're going to go to the moon! . . . And that so captured our imagination, and our emotion . . . " Charlie Mars, NASA chief lunar engineer, Kennedy Space Center from *Team Moon*

If you were one of the many people involved in planning a new space mission, what do you think would capture your imagination or emotion?

....

Hiroshima (World War II) Unit Write-to-Think

"It would be impossible to say what horrors were embedded in the minds of the children who lived through the bombing in Hiroshima. On the surface, their recollections, months after the disaster, were of an exhilarating adventure." (p. 90)

Why do you think author John Hersey chose to discuss how children experienced the bombing? How is it different from the way the adults experienced it? Why?

133

....

Stretching Beyond the Textbook © 2014 by Lauren K. Francese and Rebecca H. Marsick, Scholastic Teaching Resources

Small-Group Meetings

Throughout the coming weeks, you will be reading your book and coming to class prepared for a small-group discussion. The details below explain what you need to do.

Your tasks:

- Read the assigned pages.

- Come to class with annotations and organizer completed.

- Participate in each meeting by making constructive comments and asking questions.

What you should do while you read:

- Annotate information related to the focus question(s).

- Note unfamiliar vocabulary words and look them up.

- Reread and clarify confusing sections.

- Think of questions to share at meetings.

- Note sections that are interesting and/or important.

You will be graded based on:

- Reading and annotating the text: *Did you thoroughly annotate the text?*

- Preparing for meetings: *Did you bring your book? Did you bring your organizer?*

- Participating in meetings: *Were you on task? Did you respond to group members' questions and thoughts? Did you share your own?*

Stretching Beyond the Textbook © 2014 by Lauren K. Francese and Rebecca H. Marsick, Scholastic Teaching Resources

Teacher Scoring Chart

Student Name:
Reading (annotating text)
Preparing (organizer and book)
Participating (on task, sharing, and listening)
TOTAL:

Sample MIND Meeting Formats

Meeting Format A

ORGANIZER: WHAT'S HAPPENING? (OR WHAT'S THE BIG DEAL?)

Directions for students:

- Discuss your organizers in your group. Focus specifically on what happened in this section of text and what connections to the focus question(s) you noticed.
- As a group, choose a quote that connects to the focus question(s). Be prepared to share it with the class.

TIPS FOR TEACHERS:

In this format, students have some open time for discussion before they go back to the text and choose a quote. Move around the room and monitor students as they select their quotes. Discuss with them the connection to the focus question(s). As a wrap-up for the meetings, have each group share its quote with the whole class.

Meeting Format B

ORGANIZER: WHY DO YOU THINK THAT? (OR WHAT DOES THE TEXT SAY?)

Directions for students:

- On your own, choose a quote from the text to share with your group. Be sure you can explain how it connects to the focus question(s).
- Share your quotes together. After someone shares a quote, everyone else should share their thoughts on how that quote relates to the focus questions. You can also ask one another questions about these quotes.
- At the end of the meeting, be prepared to share *three* interesting things you talked about during your meeting.

TIPS FOR TEACHERS:

In this format, students have to search the text more independently and bring their thoughts to the group in order to engage in discussion. This is a really good format for reluctant readers. As you monitor the group meetings, you will be able to see which students annotated and thought about the text as they read. Unprepared students will be shuffling papers around and might have a harder time making the connections, a signal to you to implement appropriate reading strategies for those students.

Meeting Format C

ORGANIZER: WHAT MAKES YOU WONDER?

Directions for students:

- As a group, present questions about the text to one other. Are you wondering about an individual's motives or decision making? Have portions of the text confused you? Are there bigger questions about this topic that have come into your mind as you read the book?
- Share with your group and discuss everyone's ideas and thoughts.
- At the end of the meeting, be prepared to share *two* questions you discussed as a group.

TIPS FOR TEACHERS:

Questioning while engaging with a text can be a challenge for students. Sometimes, in groups with peers, students hesitate to ask questions because they worry about being judged. This format requires some patience and practice, especially with younger adolescents. It is especially compatible with memoirs, which typically feature a clear voice that encourages students to make personal connections and ask questions.

Stretching Beyond the Textbook © 2014 by Lauren K. Francese and Rebecca H. Marsick, Scholastic Teaching Resources

Meeting Format D

ORGANIZER: SEQUENCE OF EVENTS

Directions for students:

- Draw a picture related to an important part of the text.
- As a group, share your pictures and try to guess which portions of the text the artist is referring to.
- Once everyone has guessed (successfully or unsuccessfully), share the passage from the text that inspired the drawing.

TIPS FOR TEACHERS:

This is always a fun activity for a meeting. Most students enjoy drawing parts of the text, and the guessing game makes them really have to think about what they read. At the end of the period, you may choose to share a few drawings or have students post their drawings with the quote from the text written below it.

Meeting Format E

ORGANIZER: WHY DO YOU THINK THAT?

Directions for students:

- What surprised you while you were reading? Discuss parts of the text that made you think differently about the topic.
- As a group, identify *three* new understandings you have after reading. Be prepared to share with the whole class.

TIPS FOR TEACHERS:

This format is great for exploring informational texts in more depth. It will encourage students to point out when they've encountered new learning in the text. These new understandings can be a starting point for independent research and mini-lessons about topics that will engage students.

Meeting Format F

ORGANIZER: MULTIPLE PERSPECTIVES

Directions for students:

- Choose three people or groups from the text. Identify *each* different perspective.
- As a group, present each of the perspectives using evidence from your book.

TIPS FOR TEACHERS:

This is a great format for texts that include accounts from multiple people or that present diverse perspectives on a topic. Narrative nonfiction that describes the journey or experience of multiple people can also work well in this format.

137

Meeting Format G

ORGANIZER: EMPATHY

Directions for students:

- Try to empathize with, or "walk in the shoes" of, the people in your book. With your group, choose two people or groups and describe their situation.
- Then explain what it might be like to be in that situation. What might you be thinking about? How might you be feeling? What might you want/need/wish?
- Be prepared to share with the whole class.

TIPS FOR TEACHERS:

After reading a text, many students will reflect that they consider themselves lucky to have never experienced what the individuals or groups in their books have faced. That is not thinking deeply, that is feeling bad for someone. This puts students at a comfortable distance away from the text. Encourage them to explain what it might have been like to live like that person and to think deeply about the author's message. Was the story told just to make readers feel bad for them? Or does the author have a deeper message? This is where rich discussion develops.

Meeting Format H

ORGANIZER: WORDS FROM THE WISE

Directions for students:

- Identify important words or short phrases in the text.
- Explain the significance of these words, using evidence from the text.
- Share with your group.
- Write all your group's words on one sheet of paper and discuss connections between and among the words. What do these words have in common? What do they tell you about the topic or ideas presented in the text?

TIPS FOR TEACHERS:

Choosing just a few words encourages students to really look at the text in a different way. They have to reread text and pinpoint important words. This is crucial for developing as a reader of nonfiction. You can pair this with a mini-lesson about bias and/or author's purpose. A whole-class discussion about why authors have chosen certain words or phases or a vocabulary review of important terms related to the topic can be naturally woven into the unit, and it is completely driven by students!

138

Close Reading to Help
With Visualization

CHAPTER 1 *HIROSHIMA*

"Mr. Tanimoto was a small man, quick to talk, laugh, and cry. He wore his black hair parted in the middle and rather long; the prominence of the frontal bones just above his eyebrows and the smallness of his mustache, mouth, and chin gave him a strange, old-young look, boyish and yet wise, weak and yet fiery. He moved nervously and fast, but with a restraint which suggested that he was a cautious, thoughtful man."

1. *Highlight all the adjectives that describe Mr. Tanimoto.*

2. *Of the highlighted adjectives, underline the adjectives that describe his personality.*

3. *In your own words, what does Mr. Tanimoto look like?*

4. *Based on the paragraph above, how do you think Mr. Tanimoto will react to the dropping of the atomic bomb on his city?*

139

Name _____ Period _____ Date _____

Hiroshima Introduction

STUDENT NOTES

Japan
Where is Japan located?

The Bombing of Pearl Harbor
What was the significance of this event?

Japanese-American Internment
What actions did FDR take as a result of the attack on Pearl Harbor?

Japanese War Strategies
Why were the Japanese a difficult enemy?

American Firebombings of Japan
What did America do to respond to the Japanese strategies?

Dropping the Bomb
- *What did Truman know about the bomb prior to becoming president?*
- *How do you think this might have influenced his decision-making?*
- *Where was the bomb dropped?*
- *What was the impact of the bomb on these areas? Describe what you see in the images.*

Wrap-Up
- *What did you learn about the dropping of the atomic bomb?*
- *What perspective is presented in the reading?*

140

Close Reading of the
First Paragraph of *Hiroshima*

Read the first paragraph of *Hiroshima*.

1. *In the second sentence, place a sticky note to show where each idea should be separated. After doing this, what do you notice about the structure of this sentence?*

2. *Note the most important information that you learn about each of these six characters in the second sentence. You may only note one idea per character. In general, what information do you learn about these six characters from the second sentence?*

3. *How does the structure of this sentence help you understand these ideas?*

4. *Record the words at the end of the passage that show how the tone of the paragraph shifts.*

5. *How does the tone of the second sentence contrast with the tone at the end of the passage?*

141

Stretching Beyond the Textbook © 2014 by Lauren K. Francese and Rebecca H. Marsick, Scholastic Teaching Resources

Evidence and Inference Lesson

FOR *HIROSHIMA* (WORLD WAR II) UNIT

Lesson Objectives

- Students will define *evidence* and *inference*.

- Students will give examples of evidence and inferences and discuss making connections between the two.

- Students will apply knowledge about these terms to the current whole-class text, *Hiroshima*.

Unit Focus Questions:

- *How do people react to and recover from tragedy?*

- *What is the importance of multiple perspectives when studying history?*

Rationale/Context for the Lesson

Some students effectively use evidence but do not elaborate on their thinking, and other students share their thinking but do not use adequate evidence. Students need to see the connection between using evidence and making inferences/connections when reading and observing.

As we began the *Hiroshima* reading, this phenomenon became even clearer in student discussions. As Lauren read a section of the book about a survivor's story, she asked students to tell her the sequence of events using evidence from the text. They all jumped to the conclusion that "the bomb was dropped," even though the text does not directly state this. They were making an inference but not connecting that inference to the evidence in the text that helped them to draw that conclusion.

Monitoring/Assessment Strategies

- *Preassessment:* Use prior written work and monitoring of classroom discussion as students progress through the text to inform your teaching.

- *Ongoing:* Throughout the lesson, there will be frequent points for students to ask clarifying questions. These questions in conjunction with their work in groups will help you to adjust the lesson accordingly.

- *Postassessment:* Use the written work submitted at the end of class and application of students' ability to determine the difference between evidence and inference in the whole-class dialogue. This distinction should be evident on students' Dialogue Preparation Sheet.

142

Initiation

The lesson will begin with a warm-up asking students the following questions:

When studying a topic:

- *Where does evidence come from?*
- *Where do inferences come from?*

Students write responses in their notebooks and then share answers as a class.

Lesson Development

1. Students will write down the working definition of *evidence* and *inferences* on their handout.

2. Students will watch the Pixar short film *Partly Cloudy* and make inferences about it as they watch, citing evidence from what they are seeing to support their thinking.

3. Students will share their inferences in their groups and select one or two to share with the class.

4. Students will then apply the skill to *Hiroshima*. They will be given a handout with evidence from the text and will have to make an inference about what they are reading. They will need to highlight/underline specific pieces of evidence that support their thinking.

5. At the end of class, students will have time to work on their Dialogue Preparation Sheet and apply this skill. The application handout will be collected for further assessment of students' skill development.

Closure

Ask students to review the handout and respond to the following question: *What did you learn about the skill of inferencing today?* Collect all materials at the end of class.

Evidence and Inference Class Activity

While watching the video clip, make inferences and cite evidence to explain your thinking.

INFERENCE	EVIDENCE
I think . . .	What makes you think that?
I think . . .	What makes you think that?
I think . . .	What makes you think that?

Write a definition for each word:

Evidence:

Inference:

Name _____ Period _____ Date _____

Dialogue Preparation Sheet

HIROSHIMA (WORLD WAR II) UNIT

Use evidence from the text to brainstorm the following topics. Mark your evidence with an **E** and your inferences (*thinking*) with an **I**. Use a separate sheet of paper if necessary.

Perspective

What did you learn about perspective?

How does it relate to the study of history?

Empathy (understanding how others feel or experience an event)
What did you learn about yourself as you read this book?

Focus Question

How do people recover from tragedy?

Create three questions you would like to present during the whole-class dialogue. These questions should foster discussion, not be questions that have a simple, one-word answer.

Tip! Go through your annotations and class materials and think about some of your own personal reactions to the book. Develop questions that might allow you to see multiple perspectives and reactions about a quote or specific section of the book.

This will be turned in as part of your grade!

Name _____ Period _____ Date _____

Dialogue Preparation Sheet

SPACE RACE UNIT

Using evidence and excerpts from the text, develop questions to ask and discuss during the dialogue. Write your questions below and a brief response to each one.

This sheet will reflect your perspective, and the seminar will allow you to hear the perspectives of others and to share your thinking, too.

One World-Connection Question:

Write a question connecting the text to the real world.

Two Open-Ended Questions:

Write two questions that you have thought about while reading this book. You can go back and review your organizers, too!

Questions: Using your notes, write evidence from your book to respond to the questions below. They will be discussed during the seminar.

- *How did America's fear of Communism influence decision-making about space programs?*
- *Was competition during the Space Race a good thing or a bad thing? Why?*
- *What is the legacy of the Space Race? (How has the Space Race impacted life today?)*

This will be turned in as part of your grade!

Stretching Beyond the Textbook © 2014 by Lauren K. Francese and Rebecca H. Marsick, Scholastic Teaching Resources

Name _____ Period _____ Date _____

Dialogue Preparation Sheet

_____

Use evidence from the text to brainstorm the following topics. Mark your evidence with an **E** and your inferences (thinking) with an **I**. Use a separate sheet of paper, if necessary.

Perspective

Focus Questions

Create three questions you would like to present during the seminar. These questions should foster discussion, not be questions that have a simple, one-word answer.

Tip! Go through your annotation and class materials and think about some of your own personal reactions to the book. Develop questions that might allow you to see multiple perspectives and reactions about a quote or specific section of the book.

This will be turned in as part of your grade!

Scoring Sheet

This chart is a helpful tool for scripting and making notes during the dialogue. The "Score" column correlates with the Dialogue Grading Rubric, so it is easy to mark students' score for each category as Beginning, Developing, Accomplished, or Exemplary.

STUDENT NAME	NOTES	SCORE
		Uses Evidence: B D A E Contributes: B D A E Collaborates: B D A E
		Uses Evidence: B D A E Contributes: B D A E Collaborates: B D A E
		Uses Evidence: B D A E Contributes: B D A E Collaborates: B D A E
		Uses Evidence: B D A E Contributes: B D A E Collaborates: B D A E
		Uses Evidence: B D A E Contributes: B D A E Collaborates: B D A E
		Uses Evidence: B D A E Contributes: B D A E Collaborates: B D A E
		Uses Evidence: B D A E Contributes: B D A E Collaborates: B D A E
		Uses Evidence: B D A E Contributes: B D A E Collaborates: B D A E
		Uses Evidence: B D A E Contributes: B D A E Collaborates: B D A E

Dialogue Grading Rubric

	BEGINNING *5 points*	DEVELOPING *6 points*	ACCOMPLISHED *8 points*	EXEMPLARY *10 points*
The student gives evidence and makes inferences/connections during the discussion. The student poses questions that connect the ideas of several students and responds to others' questions and comments with relevant evidence, observations, and ideas.				
The student contributes by sharing thoughts, questions, and ideas that are on task and focused. The student acknowledges new information expressed by others and can explain, clarify, or revise his or her own views in light of the evidence presented.				
The student behaves appropriately, actively listens, and makes positive contributions to a collaborative classroom environment. The student can follow rules for the class dialogue and decision-making to fully participate.				
The student comes to the class dialogue prepared, having read the text, and can explicitly draw on that preparation by referring to evidence to probe and reflect on ideas under discussion. *The Dialogue Preparation Sheet is graded for this category.*				

149

Sample Guided Reflection

HIROSHIMA (WORLD WAR II) UNIT

This reflection is between you and your teacher. You should feel safe to share your thoughts, opinions, and ideas. I want to hear them!

Use your notes from class and the Dialogue Preparation Sheet to complete the planning outline below. Bring this to class with you tomorrow. You will have time to type your final reflection in class tomorrow.

1. Respond to the focus question: *What do multiple perspectives show us about how people deal with tragedy?*

2. In one or two words or a short statement, how would you describe your experience reading and discussing this book over the last two weeks? Explain using specific examples from the book *and* discussion.

3. What did you learn about perspectives? How did seeing multiple perspectives shape/influence your thinking?

4. Talk about book-group discussion and the final seminar. Describe your experience. Use evidence from the book and discussion to support your thinking.

5. When you finish writing your reflection, create a title. The title must include the word (or words) you chose to describe your experience.

Stretching Beyond the Textbook © 2014 by Lauren K. Francese and Rebecca H. Marsick, Scholastic Teaching Resources

Name _____ Period _____ Date _____

Sample Guided Reflection

SPACE RACE UNIT

This reflection is between you and your teacher. You should feel safe to share your thoughts, opinions, and ideas. I want to hear them!

Use your notes from class and your Dialogue Preparation Sheet to complete the planning outline below. Bring this to class with you tomorrow. You will have time to type your final reflection in class tomorrow.

1. *Reflection Title*
   Develop a creative title for your outline that summarizes in a few words your experience reading about the Space Race.

2. *Introductory Quote*
   Choose a powerful quote (cite the page number) from your book that was meaningful to you and relates to the focus questions.

3. *Response to the Reflection Question*
   When Neil Armstrong set foot on the moon, he said, "That's one small step for man, one giant leap for mankind." Was it? Use evidence from your book and the seminar to explain your thinking.

4. *Description of Book Club Experience*
   Clearly describe your group reading experience. How did the discussions go? Did you feel that you chose an appropriate-level text? What were some of the best/worst parts of the experience? What will you do to enhance or improve your experience next time?

5. *Description of Dialogue Experience*
   Explain how the dialogue went for you. Did you participate? Were there challenges for you during the dialogue? What might you do differently next time?

6. *"Moving Forward" Concluding Sentence*
   End your reflection with a sentence (or two) that states your plan/goal for developing as a reader of nonfiction. Here are some things to think about:
   - *Are there things you need to improve or work on as a reader?*
   - *Have you come to better understand the purpose for reading nonfiction?*
   - *Has reading nonfiction challenged your thinking in new ways?*

151

Hiroshima Character Bookmark

Copy this sheet on cardstock. Cut apart the bookmarks and give one to each student.

MISS TOSHIKO SASAKI—(*not related to Dr. Sasaki*) spends much time in hospital due to an injured leg she suffered during the A-bomb attack; this injury would cause her to suffer for the rest of her life. As a result, she becomes a nun to dedicate her life to helping others. She lived up to the comment that, "One should only look forward and never back to give one's life meaning."

DR. MASAKAZU FUJII—doctor with compassion but enjoys a life of wealth. He had moved his family out of Hiroshima out of fear before bombing. He is forced to work harder after the bombing. He later develops cancer and is forced to face his own mortality.

MRS. HATSUYO NAKAMURA—a woman troubled before the bombing by the loss of her husband while serving in the army in 1942 and is deeply concerned for her children after the bombing. With respect to the bombing, she embraced the Japanese concept of, "It can't be helped." She symbolized the many Japanese for whom the bomb was not personal.

FATHER WILHELM KLEINSORGE—a German priest who leads a life of selflessness, sacrificing his own health to help others. He goes for days at a time with little sleep to treat the wounded even though he deals with radiation illness. At the end of his life, many travel to see him and thank him.

DR. TERUFUMI SASAKI—(*not related to Toshiko Sasaki*) a young surgeon for the Red Cross Hospital and the only unhurt doctor. He works tirelessly to treat the wounded. He is haunted after the bombing. The Japanese culture believes in burying the dead respectfully so he is haunted by all the bodies that will not be buried and those he could not help. "Dr. Sasaki lost all sense of profession and stopped working as a skillful surgeon and sympathetic man; he became an automaton . . ." p. 26.

REVEREND KIYOSHI TANIMOTO—displays endless passion, which is often confronted by feelings of helplessness and rage. For days, he physically carries people, rows boats, organizes people, and rescues people from the river. Some of the people he rescues end up drowning. It is important to him that people showed the spirit of the ancestors by "dying well."

152

MISS TOSHIKO SASAKI—(*not related to Dr. Sasaki*) spends much time in hospital due to an injured leg she suffered during the A-bomb attack; this injury would cause her to suffer for the rest of her life. As a result, she becomes a nun to dedicate her life to helping others. She lived up to the comment that, "One should only look forward and never back to give one's life meaning."

DR. MASAKAZU FUJII—doctor with compassion but enjoys a life of wealth. He had moved his family out of Hiroshima out of fear before bombing. He is forced to work harder after the bombing. He later develops cancer and is forced to face his own mortality.

MRS. HATSUYO NAKAMURA—a woman troubled before the bombing by the loss of her husband while serving in the army in 1942 and is deeply concerned for her children after the bombing. With respect to the bombing, she embraced the Japanese concept of, "It can't be helped." She symbolized the many Japanese for whom the bomb was not personal.

FATHER WILHELM KLEINSORGE—a German priest who leads a life of selflessness, sacrificing his own health to help others. He goes for days at a time with little sleep to treat the wounded even though he deals with radiation illness. At the end of his life, many travel to see him and thank him.

DR. TERUFUMI SASAKI—(*not related to Toshiko Sasaki*) a young surgeon for the Red Cross Hospital and the only unhurt doctor. He works tirelessly to treat the wounded. He is haunted after the bombing. The Japanese culture believes in burying the dead respectfully so he is haunted by all the bodies that will not be buried and those he could not help. "Dr. Sasaki lost all sense of profession and stopped working as a skillful surgeon and sympathetic man; he became an automaton . . ." p. 26.

REVEREND KIYOSHI TANIMOTO—displays endless passion, which is often confronted by feelings of helplessness and rage. For days, he physically carries people, rows boats, organizes people, and rescues people from the river. Some of the people he rescues end up drowning. It is important to him that people showed the spirit of the ancestors by "dying well."

MISS TOSHIKO SASAKI—(*not related to Dr. Sasaki*) spends much time in hospital due to an injured leg she suffered during the A-bomb attack; this injury would cause her to suffer for the rest of her life. As a result, she becomes a nun to dedicate her life to helping others. She lived up to the comment that, "One should only look forward and never back to give one's life meaning."

DR. MASAKAZU FUJII—doctor with compassion but enjoys a life of wealth. He had moved his family out of Hiroshima out of fear before bombing. He is forced to work harder after the bombing. He later develops cancer and is forced to face his own mortality.

MRS. HATSUYO NAKAMURA—a woman troubled before the bombing by the loss of her husband while serving in the army in 1942 and is deeply concerned for her children after the bombing. With respect to the bombing, she embraced the Japanese concept of, "It can't be helped." She symbolized the many Japanese for whom the bomb was not personal.

FATHER WILHELM KLEINSORGE—a German priest who leads a life of selflessness, sacrificing his own health to help others. He goes for days at a time with little sleep to treat the wounded even though he deals with radiation illness. At the end of his life, many travel to see him and thank him.

DR. TERUFUMI SASAKI—(*not related to Toshiko Sasaki*) a young surgeon for the Red Cross Hospital and the only unhurt doctor. He works tirelessly to treat the wounded. He is haunted after the bombing. The Japanese culture believes in burying the dead respectfully so he is haunted by all the bodies that will not be buried and those he could not help. "Dr. Sasaki lost all sense of profession and stopped working as a skillful surgeon and sympathetic man; he became an automaton . . ." p. 26.

REVEREND KIYOSHI TANIMOTO—displays endless passion, which is often confronted by feelings of helplessness and rage. For days, he physically carries people, rows boats, organizes people, and rescues people from the river. Some of the people he rescues end up drowning. It is important to him that people showed the spirit of the ancestors by "dying well."

Name _____ Period _____ Date _____

Hiroshima: Chapter _____

Level 1

As you read *Hiroshima*, follow *Miss Sasaki* as she experiences this event. Update the chart below as you read. Bring your book and the chart with you to class every day.

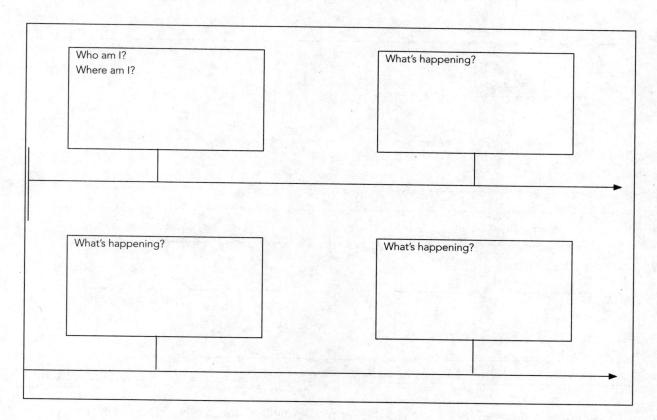

Who am I?
Where am I?

What's happening?

What's happening?

What's happening?

How is *Miss Sasaki* reacting to or recovering from this tragedy? Explain in three or four sentences using evidence from the chapter. You may paraphrase or use quotes.

Hiroshima: Chapter _____

Level 2

As you read *Hiroshima*, follow *Father Wilhelm Kleinsorge* and *Reverend Kiyoshi Tanimoto* as they experience this event. Update the chart below as you read. Bring your book and the chart with you to class every day.

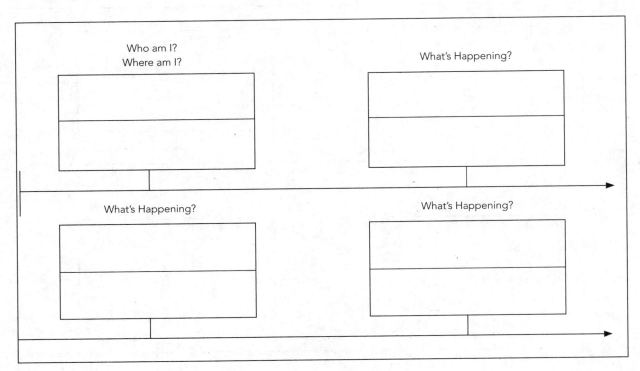

How is *Father Wilhelm Kleinsorge* reacting to or recovering from this tragedy? Explain in three or four sentences using evidence from the chapter. You may paraphrase or use quotes.

How is *Reverend Kiyoshi Tanimoto* reacting to or recovering from this tragedy? Explain in three or four sentences using evidence from the chapter. You may paraphrase or use quotes.

154

Hiroshima: Chapter _____

Level 3

As you read *Hiroshima*, follow *all of the characters* and compare their journeys as they experience this event. Update the chart below as you read. Bring your book and the chart with you to class every day.

CHARACTER	WHO AM I? WHERE AM I?	WHAT'S HAPPENING?
MISS SASAKI		
DR. FUJII		
MRS. NAKAMURA		
FATHER KLEINSORGE		
DR. SASAKI		
REVEREND TANIMOTO		

How are these individuals reacting to or recovering from this tragedy? Choose *3 people* and explain in three or four sentences using evidence from the chapter. You may paraphrase or use quotes.

155

Stretching Beyond the Textbook © 2014 by Lauren K. Francese and Rebecca H. Marsick, Scholastic Teaching Resources

MIND Unit Planner

CCSS:		
Goals and Objectives	Unit goal:	
	Objectives for direct instruction:	
	Objectives for book-group experience:	
Focus Question(s) *All areas may not apply for the unit. Choose one that works to achieve your curricular goal.*	My life question:	
	Understanding/empathy question:	
	Global citizenship question:	
Assessments *Indicate formative (F) or summative (S)*	Graphic organizer:	
	Pre-test:	
	Socratic seminar:	
	Posttest:	
	Written work:	
	Presentation:	
Differentiation	Process:	
	Product:	
	Content:	
Book Choices	Narrative text:	
	Informational text:	
	Historical fiction paired with a nonfiction informational text:	
	Graphic novels:	
Calendar/Timing	# of book-group meetings:	
	# of strategy-based mini-lessons:	
	# of content-based mini-lessons:	
	# of days for culminating Socratic seminar:	

MIND Unit Planner

BOOK-GROUP EXPERIENCE UNIT PLANNER: Multiple Perspectives and the Atomic Bomb—Whole-Class Text

Goals and Objectives	Unit goal: Students will engage in thoughtful dialogue about multiple perspectives in history using evidence from text. (CCSS: Integration of Knowledge and Ideas)
	Objectives for direct instruction:
	−Students will describe the sequence of events for people in Hiroshima. (CCSS: Key Ideas and Details and Craft and Structure)
	Objectives for book-group experience:
	−Students will identify multiple perspectives within a nonfiction text.
	−Students will reflect on diverse perspectives and how they shape history.
	−Students will analyze the impact of multiple perspectives on the nations' (America and Japan) reaction to tragedy. (CCSS: Integration of Knowledge and Ideas)
Focus Question(s) All areas may not apply for the unit. Choose one that works to achieve your curricular goal.	My life question: What is perspective? How does perspective shape/influence your world?
	Understanding/empathy question: How do people respond to a tragedy or disaster?
	Global citizenship question: What do multiple perspectives show us about how people deal with tragedy?
Assessments Indicate formative (F) or summative (S)	Reading organizer: F
	Preassessment: Anticipation Guide and Preassessment F
	Whole class dialogue: S
	Posttest: S
	Written work: Write-to-Thinks (F) and Reflection (S)

continued on next page

Stretching Beyond the Textbook © 2014 by Lauren K. Francese and Rebecca H. Marsick, Scholastic Teaching Resources

Differentiation	Process: Students will be provided differentiated organizers. 3– All six perspectives 2– Compare and contrast Reverend Tanimoto and Father Kleinsorge 1– Follow the story of Miss Sasaki Content: There are SIX perspectives in the book. Level 1 students will read for all six perspectives (the whole book) and Avalon Project excerpts, Level 2 students will read two perspectives and compare them throughout and read Avalon Project excepts, and Level 3 students will read one perspective and make connections/ comparisons to the supplementary materials: Yale Avalon Project Excerpts.
Book Choices	Narrative nonfiction text: <u>Hiroshima</u>, John Hersey Informational text: Class Notes/Introductory Materials, <u>Yale Avalon Project Excerpts</u> Historical fiction paired with a nonfiction informational text: none Graphic novels: none
Calendar/Timing	# of book-group meetings: 4 # of strategy-based mini-lessons: 3–20 Questions, Close Reading and Annotating Text # of content-based mini-lessons: 2 days intro notes, 1 day science/technology of the bomb with Science teacher # of days for culminating dialogue: 1 class period for planning/prep, 1 class period for dialogue

MIND Unit Planner

CLAUDETTE COLVIN: TWICE TOWARD JUSTICE Whole-Class Text

Goals and Objectives	Unit goal: **Students will evaluate the role of young people in social change and discuss how social change developed and evolved in the modern civil rights movement.** (CCSS Integration of Knowledge and Ideas)
	Objectives for direct instruction:
	-Students will analyze the importance of the Brown vs. Board of Education case.
	-Students will discuss the role of Rosa Parks in the Montgomery Bus Boycott.
	-Students will describe how Martin Luther King, Jr. became the leader of the modern civil rights movement. (CCSS Key Ideas and Details)
	Objectives for book-group experience:
	-Students will compare the stories of Rosa Parks and Claudette Colvin.
	-Students will reflect on the role of young people in the movement.
	-Students will evaluate the leadership and the social change in the civil rights movement.
	(CCSS Integration of Knowledge and Ideas)
Focus Question(s) All areas may not apply for the unit. Choose one that works to achieve your curricular goal.	My life question: Do young people have the power to inspire change? Understanding/empathy question: Is it okay to break the rules sometimes? Global citizenship question: What is the importance of leadership in a movement that is pushing for social change?
Assessments Indicate formative (F) or summative (S)	Graphic organizer: **F** Preassessment: Rosa, By Nikki Giovanni Read-Aloud and Anticipation Guide: **F** Whole Class Dialogue: **S** Posttest: Anticipation Guide Activity (S) Written work: **Differentiated Writing Assignments** (S)

continued on next page

Stretching Beyond the Textbook © 2014 by Lauren K. Francese and Rebecca H. Marsick, Scholastic Teaching Resources

Differentiation	Process: Students will read and complete organizers for their selected level. Product: Student organizers will be provided at three levels and final written work will be leveled as well. Content: ALL students will be reading the same text for this unit.
Book Choices	Narrative text: Twice Toward Justice: Claudette Colvin, Phillip Hoose Rosa, Nikki Giovanni Informational text: Class Notes/Introductory Materials Historical fiction paired with a nonfiction informational text: Girl Who Fell From the Sky, Heidi Durrow (Level 2 only)
Calendar/Timing	# of book-group meetings: 5 # of strategy-based mini-lessons: Write-to-Think, Sequence of Events # of content-based mini-lessons: Content Lessons throughout # of days for culminating Socratic seminar: 1 class period planning/prep, 1 class period for dialogue